STAND

*Bringing African Women's Rights
into the Modern Age*

DR. HILDA M. K. TADRIA

MEMPROW FOUNDER

Co-Founder, African Women's Development Fund

Published by Hilda M. K. Tadria and Action Wealth Publishing.

Kemp House
152 -160 City Road
London, EC1V 2NX
United Kingdom

ISBN: 978-1-914994-10-4

Printed and bound in the United Kingdom.

This book is dedicated to several people:

To my parents, George William, and Justine Faith Kabushenga, (R.I.P.) for steering me in the right direction with unconditional tough love.

To my husband, Constantine Aliakai D. Tadria, (R.I.P.) for letting me be with no perhaps, ifs or buts.

My children, Patrice and Vanessa, whose courage to take on and adjust to new challenges, including parents who lived outside general gender social norms, continues to amaze me. And to Grace, my son's wife, who brought into our home three gifts in one: a daughter and wonderful daughter-in law, as well as her full family of cheerleaders to me.

To my grandchildren Nelson, Letaasi, Onabikoa, Oluwaseyi, Pitiki and Kayode for accepting me as a I am, a feminist who they know as a 'grandmother with the biggest number of gadgets who is always travelling. To all my nephews and nieces for maintaining faith in me.

To my feminist sisters, as well as the girls and young women of the world, for bringing meaning to all I do.

CONTENTS

HILDA M. K. TADRIA

ACKNOWLEDGEMENTS

MY LIFE WAS SHAPED by amazing people, in addition to my parents. My teachers stand out as people who nurtured me and my free spirit at different stages of my primary and secondary schooling, at university and even in my post-graduate education. They always looked for and brought out the best in me; never once did I feel diminished by my teachers even when I got it wrong.

I know I would be telling a different tale if it was not for these teachers. I want to name a few whose impact on me left a permanent mark of faith in myself. I want to acknowledge Ms. Constance Hornby, a Missionary to Uganda during World War II, who on her arrival sought out girls, including my mother, and gave them an opportunity for education; I believe she started this. She was also my first teacher when I was five years old. I still remember her kindness.

My early education life was greatly impacted by my primary school Mathematics and English teacher, Erina Lushaya, and personal mentor, Omukuru Losira Namatovu, together with my junior secondary school teacher, Ms. Ely, all of whom made no room for shoddy work. My senior secondary school life was packed with teachers who had more faith in me than I had in myself. The wonderful Miss Joan Cox, a Headmistress of Gayaza for many years, believed I was dramatically oriented and could act in school plays; as a result, she never left me out of school performances, elocution competitions, or early-morning Scripture readings during school assembly; all of which contributed to taking away my fear of speaking in public.

I acknowledge Ms. Sheelagh Warren, who saved me from myself by convincing me I was made for University when I was opting out for a college diploma. It is through her conviction that I agreed to apply to join Makerere University, where at that time (1967) I met a young lecturer, Adam Kuiper, who taught social anthropology with so much conviction and enthusiasm that he instilled in me an equal passion for the subject. When he told me I was material for graduate studies at Cambridge University, I knew there was no room for failure, only a first class would do.

Getting to Minnesota University is also a result of having been at Cambridge University but through another team of teachers: Professor Herbert and Anne Pick, whom I met in Makerere, where they spent a year teaching. In Minnesota, Professor Gudeman, Professor Susan Geiger, and Professor Janet Spector took me on an amazing journey of discovery of the link between economics and women's work, as well as the power of patriarchy in the lives of men and women alike. I want to acknowledge these teachers and all those I have not mentioned by name and thank all of them, because they never let me settle for less than the best.

Between them, they set the ground rules for my performance, which kept me on top of my game, including my profession, at different times.

I want to acknowledge my network of feminist friends, many of whom always tell me they want to be like me when they grow up; and yet they are already like me, or rather, I am like them. Friends, you know who you are. I thank you for constantly validating me and what I bring to the table. You have contributed to my strength in defying patriarchal norms and definitions of a woman.

My life's journey, I strongly believe, would have taken a different trajectory somewhere down the road if it were not for some of my lifelong personal friends: Philomena Amoako, Anne, and Herbert (R.I.P.), Hannah Stanton (R.I.P), Margaret Bott, and a relatively newer friend Susie Johnson, all of whom contributed in an incredibly defining and special way to the fulfilment of my aspirations at different times in my life.

I met the then Philomena Ansah from Ghana in Cambridge in 1970, where by sheer accident we found ourselves in the same house at Newnham College, Cambridge. We were two young African women, a very rare breed in Cambridge at the time, confronting a new and very different culture, and I must say I was the greener of the two. Philomena, in her unassuming subtle ways, taught me the dos and don'ts of survival in the foreign and highly competitive culture we found ourselves in. We formed a permanent friendship that has stood the test of time, and she may not know it, but she opened doors to life-changing opportunities that I never dreamed of.

Margaret Bott, then Pemberton, was a young woman travelling in East Africa when she found herself in Uganda without a friend. She had gravitated to Makerere, and we met somewhere in my final year (1969-1970) at a popular bench for socialising among residents of Mary Stuart, also my hall of residence. She herself had just finished university in England and on learning that, Hannah Stanton our Hall Warden insisted we meet, because I was going to that famous university, Cambridge. We have been friends since then. Margaret Bott gave me my first induction into Cambridge culture. Later on, in 1981, when she and Hannah learned I was about to turn down an opportunity to study at the University of Minnesota, they rallied. Although I had been offered a great scholarship by the Rockefeller Foundation, it covered dependants only if one was able to pay for their relocation. On my lecturer's and my husband's even more meagre civil service salary at the time, we did not have enough resources to pay for and go with my children. When Margaret and Hannah heard of that, they put together enough ticket money to ensure I could go with the children. That is a generosity I can never forget nor repay; it is because of this that I was able to complete my studies in Minnesota and maintain sanity.

I found myself at the University of Minnesota because of Anne and Herb Pick, who had impressed me with the simple way they lived their lives, accepting everyone without judgement. They had a housekeeper whose four daughters shared a bedroom with their two daughters. Anne Pick shared cigarettes with Abooki, her housekeeper. Anyone who knows Uganda will know how expatriates and the privileged class treat their support staff, those who actually make it possible for them to continue living in privilege. They will understand why the Picks stood out as special people who became great friends for me. They left Uganda in the early seventies, but we kept in touch. When I asked them to recommend a university for my Ph.D. studies later in the eighties, they asked me to join them in Minnesota. I could not have been happier. In them, I found a strong support, a family away from home. I did not know what to expect when I went there, but winter in Minnesota was beyond expected. I survived it because of Anne and Herb, as we knew him. Herbert taught my children how to skate and toboggan in snow and to love it. He weathered snow storms to take us grocery shopping when very few dared go on the streets. Their kindness was beyond measure.

My dream of starting a mentoring and empowerment programme for young women, popularly known as MEMPROW, took on a new and practical meaning when I met Susie Johnson in the later years of my life, sometime in 2003. We had been having a long chat about future dreams after an AWDF board meeting, and I shared my idea of starting a mentoring programme after my retirement. As we stood to go to our rooms, Susie looked at me and, with her endearing chuckle, said, "I will be putting in a little money in MEMPROW starting now, so that when you are ready, no matter when, you have a small grant to help with the logistics of starting an organisation." Truth be told, it is this act of faith in my dream that encouraged me to step out and start an organisation with a grant of US$7,000 only. Another generosity I can neither repay nor forget.

It is rare to have development partners who buy into your dream and ideas without imposing a "tyranny of their expertise."[1] Over the last twelve years during which I led the organisation, MEMPROW has been supported by such partners, among them notably: African Women Development Fund (AWDF), Global Fund for Women, Mama Cash, Comic Relief, Medical Mondiale, American Jewish World Service (AJWS), Open Society Foundation (East Africa), and our first funder, United Methodist Women, Masimanyane Women's Rights International, Agent Action Fund Africa and United States Artists for Africa. These partners have supported our daring work with sustained grants. This has in turn enabled us to deepen our work and make meaningful impacts. I would like to

---

[1] William Earsterly, *The Tyrany of Experts:. Economists, Dictators, and the Forgotten Rights of the Poor*. In his book, Easterly discusses the tragedy of externally imposed development solutions provided by expatriates against indigenous knowledge and rights. He discusses what he calls "conscious direction" by experts versus "spontaneous evolution" in development that is endogenous. Authoritarian development is based on the belief that the experts advising the autocrats know better than poor individuals how to solve their problems. The support for an authoritarian approach to development is sometimes not overt but implied.

"Authoritarian development is also a pragmatic tragedy. History and modern experience suggest that free individuals with political and economic rights—call it free development—make up a remarkably successful problem-solving system. Free development gives us the right to choose amongst a myriad of spontaneous problem-solvers, rewarding those that solve our problems. These public and private problem-solvers accomplish far more than dictators who implement solutions provided by experts. We will see how free development allows the squeaky wheel to get the grease, while authoritarian development silences the squeaky wheel." (p. 12).

thank in a special way Medica Mondiale, Open Society Foundation (East Africa), AWDF, and the AJWS who invested in our change management process and thereby brought our succession plans into fruitful success. AWDF and OSIEA supported the writing and publication of this book. In recognition of this, any proceeds from the book will go into MEMPROW's sustainability account.

Lastly, I want to acknowledge, not only the unqualified support to my feminist journey given by my husband and children for accepting me exactly as I am, but especially for agreeing to travel on this journey with me. When you live outside the accepted social norms, you can easily be rejected by your nearest and dearest. But they have travelled with me, and my husband was always keen to keep me on the straight-and-narrow path of feminism and professionalism. He did this in many different ways, but mostly he lived it.

My husband and I met at Cambridge University in England in 1970 and got married in 1972, in the early years of the Idi Amin regime. I was by then a lecturer at Makerere University, commuting from Namulonge Research Station, where my husband was the Cotton Breeder. Every day, in order to get to Makerere in time for my lectures, I needed to get up and be out of the house by 5.30 a.m. to catch the only bus of the day at 6.00 a.m. I would then get back at 6.00 p.m. and rush to the kitchen to start making dinner, having left instructions with my support team at home that I would be the one to cook dinner.

I was newly married and still a slave to the patriarchal mind-set of a good wife; cooking for the husband is one of the prescribed roles I was told I needed to fulfil. In my second week of marriage (there were no honeymoons in those days), I came back on a Monday evening and rushed to change into my "kitchen work clothes." My husband surprised me by blocking me from entering the kitchen and asked what I wanted in the kitchen. I replied that I was going to make dinner, because I knew no one had cooked. With a huge smile on his face, he asked me why we had employed a housekeeper who was also a trained cook.

"Our relationship is not based on whether you cook or not. We must have time for conversation, but you must also have time to recover from the day, so you can perform better in your work."

The proof that his enduring support was from the heart came when I received an invitation and support from the Makerere Research Institute, where I worked at the time, to attend an international academic conference that would take place in the Netherlands; exactly 8 weeks after the birth of our second child. I came home from Work and told my husband I had just turned down the invitation to a conference because I did not think I could leave the baby so early. I remember he paused for a moment, a habit he had when presented with a dilemma, then he spoke. "You know if you do not take this invitation you will lose all opportunities. They will make an assumption that you cannot participate in academic life fully because you have children. You will never have other opportunities. You go and attend the conference and I will take care of the baby."

When we shared this decision with others, he faced a barrage of questions. They wanted to know whether his mother or my mother would come to look after the baby.

He did not pay attention to his colleagues and peers who wanted to know what he would do with a new born baby. They wanted to know whether his mother or my mother would come to look after the baby. "What does my mother, or her mother know about my baby that I do not know?" he asked.

He stood up against patriarchal expectations of a so-called "real man" and put an end to the peer pressure on him to start behaving like a patriarchal man and hand over his baby to women who knew nothing about her. From that day onwards, I knew I was free to live a life I had chosen, with no buts or ifs. Throughout my life, I have been a beneficiary of great love, kindness, and generosity; I stand tall because of that, and I am grateful.

INTRODUCTION

IT TOOK ME A LONG TIME to get to the point of writing this book. For many years, colleagues, friends, and family urged me to write. "I have no story to tell that is different from other women," was always my response.

Even when I started seeing my name and work being quoted in other people's research reports, I never thought there was a need to write. I have authored many papers; my Ph.D. thesis was used as a reference for students in gender studies in Makerere University; I am quick to put pen to paper when I read an article in the newspapers that attacks or diminishes women. It is not because I have no ability to write that I have no book to my name, until now. At one time, tired of my excuse of lack of time to write, my husband, always my cheerleader, gave me the title of what my book should be. This motivated me to start working on the outline of the book. It was immediately misplaced, never to be found, but not intentionally.

The awakening came when I started my work with the Mentoring and Empowerment Programme for Young Women (MEMPROW), an organisation for mentoring girls and young women that my husband and I started in 2008. We started using storytelling to encourage girls and women to tell their stories in order to move from a point of low self-worth to the point where they would learn how to deal with their defining experiences.

When we started working with communities, the storytelling approach was applied in working with women, so they could understand how patriarchy[2] works in their lives. When we began doing this, we were able to understand how girls and women are taught to normalise violence in their lives. I also learned to appreciate that they had new challenges in patriarchy that they were dealing with, but for which they were unprepared, like most of us. Many of the young women and boys were living under incredibly challenging conditions, with guardians and

---

[2] I use the word "patriarchy" to refer to a social system based on hierarchical social relations with hierarchy in which power is held by men, and through cultural norms and customs that favour men, withhold opportunity from women, and facilitate violence against women and girls. Patriarchy is characterized by male identification, with masculinity and male-centeredness as the core value of society: meaning that cultural ideas about what is good, desirable, and normal are usually associated with masculinity and the focus of attention is on boys/men and what they do. Patriarchy is also obsessed with control, where the only way men maintain their privileges is by controlling women. The qualities assumed to be possessed by men mark them as in control and privileged.

Patriarchal is also characterised by what Robert Wyrod, in his book, *On Aids and Masculinity in the African City* (p. 28) describes as "hegemonic masculinity," which encompasses the male as an economic provider; male authority in the home; and masculine control is most observable in the control on women's sexuality and reproductive rights, where in addition, "male sexuality is equated with sexual virility, freedom, and control." I see these as the root causes of pervasive gender inequality that is deeply entrenched patriarchy.

stepparents or distant relatives. Most of them were simply surviving, with hardly any social survival skills, and they were angry. I quickly realised that what I had perceived as a generation gap in the way we meet challenges was a consequence of their life experiences; mostly of violence of all forms within a patriarchal setting that leaves no woman unchallenged by the system. They had exceptionally low self-esteem and low aspirations as a result of the negative messaging of who they were from their guardians, stepparents, and even parents. In a discussion with one group of young women about how they handle conflict in their lives, I was shocked when I was told that the only way they solve their problem is to "fight until you see blood."

In the eleven years I have worked with girls and young women as well as boys, encouraging them to tell their stories and move on, I have lived to see them bloom with self-confidence and positive self-esteem. But I have also been asked many times, "How have you done it in your personal life, working with the challenges of trying to change entrenched negative norms and thinking about women?"

Once, in a conversation about my life with a man I though was well educated, he asked me who my "witch doctor" was. According to him, I seemed to have everything and yet I was a woman; and he did not say it as a joke. I knew he would not understand if I tried to explain my constant battle with patriarchal barriers. I realised then that I had a story to tell.

Not long ago, I finally met somebody (a man) on a mission with a passion for publishing people's stories, who was able to convince me that if I did not write my story, others would write it for me. That includes those who believe that good things only came to me, a woman, from the use of a "witch doctor." But much more importantly, Geoffrey Semaganda was able to make me understand that those who do not share their life experiences have no right to talk or complain about "how things have changed," whether for good or bad. I finally realised that sharing my life experiences, of standing up for my rights and those of other women and of challenging the accepted gender norms around a woman's place and patriarchal negative norms, is a responsibility.

STAND is written to share my feminist[3] journey and experiences of how I have been challenged and stood firmly for my rights, as well as about the forces that enabled me to defy patriarchy, a system that sets up women to collude in self-oppression or to fail; and nothing more. It does not matter whether they have all that it takes to stand or not. It is a book for all those women who, like me are struggling to stand for our rights and gender justice. And for those on the edge, trying to take a firm stand, to be aware of the systemic ways in which women are oppressed, so as not to fall off.

---

[3] Feminism means different things to different people, but to all diverse meanings it is a "theory of equality" (Owen M. Fiss, *What is Feminism?* 1 Jan 1994) and stands for equality between women and men. I have attempted to put this into reality by challenging discrimination and subordination in patriarchy. At MEMPROW, we challenge not just discrimination as it focuses on individuals but on subordination of women, which is institutionalised in patriarchal systems and norms. We therefore work towards dismantling these.

I want to assure the girls and young women who read this book that it is not because they are not standing firm for their rights that they are under oppression; but rather because the system in which we fight for our rights is biased against us. The reason for my success at what I have set myself to do—freeing myself—is nothing to do with witchcraft. It is not that I stood up differently or better than other women who are always standing up. I believe it is because I finally understood the power of patriarchy on my life and on other women's lives. Looking back, I recognise the same fights my mother fought and appreciate what I learned from her.

Paul Freire, the author of *Pedagogy of the Oppressed,* says, "The comprehension of oppression is 'indispensable' to a new vision of the world based on justice and freedom." In my case, I can say with certainty that it is this comprehension of oppression that freed me and enabled me to defy patriarchy.

To the girls and young women, I hope you will learn and have the courage to take a stand whenever you can and must. But first, you have to recognise and understand where the oppression is coming from. I hope my story will help you to understand and deal with your oppression; to stand with confidence and believe that a different and better life is possible, contrary to what patriarchy tells you. I believe that the "#MeToo" campaign is the greatest awakening to the power of patriarchy in women's lives. You too can be part of the story of *Stand.*

Writing this book has also given me an opportunity for self-assessment. "Have I served my purpose on Earth?" is a question I had to ask myself. In this book, I will share specific examples of what I have brought to the table and how I have used my talents, not only as I see it but through other people's eyes, as well.

CHAPTER ONE

BACKGROUND

I WAS BORN AT THE CLOSE of World War II, a baby boomer, to parents whose generation has been described as "builders."[4] Michael McQueen describes this generation as DUTIFUL, FRUGAL, STOIC, and PROPER. These are characteristics that describe my parents aptly. My parents were also of a generation of men and women who understood colonialism well and fought for independence. My parents were both very politically conscious; they knew about and talked to us about the Belgians in Congo, our neighbours, and how a great man named Patrice Lumumba was expected to take over leadership.

Patrice Émery Lumumba was born in 1925, a few months before my mother. He was a Congolese politician and independence leader who served as the first Prime Minister of the independent Democratic Republic of the Congo from June until September 1960. They saw him as a man of their generation and a beacon of hope at the time

---

[4] Michael McQueen. *The New Rules of Engagement: A Guide to Understanding & Connecting with Generation Y*, 2011.

Uganda was working for its independence. It is not by coincidence that our first child is named Patrice after Lumumba. My parents understood that information is power and in the 1950s, invested in purchasing a radio. They expected us children to sit quietly with them and listen to the British Broadcasting Corporation news before bed and at dawn.

Both of my parents lived well into their late eighties. In their book, there was no shade of grey in truth. It was either black or white. My father never stopped telling us that "a liar and a thief are one and the same person." They made it clear, both in action and words, that hard work paid off, and they found pleasure in whatever work they did. They both rebranded themselves as entrepreneurs when my father retired from public civil service work. When we were growing up, my mother made it clear there would be no benefits in terms of food, at the end of the day, if you did not work during that day. She had no hesitation in sending a child to bed without dinner, if she was convinced the child had produced nothing during the day. The exception was if she saw you spending your time reading books; and that is where I invested most of my time.

My parents were not completely poor, but all of us children spent our primary school days walking miles to school without shoes. My parents reasoning being that if no other children had shoes, what made us different to assume we had to have shoes? My parents believed in living within their means, and my father's popular response any time we asked for something he knew he could not afford was,

"Oteine teitwa," literally translated means "no one gets killed for what they do not have."

I was the second-born child and the only girl among three boys for a long time. I held a special place as the only girl, but as a girl I was also treated as a leader to be held responsible for both good and bad. My mother made it clear I was responsible for keeping law and order and for ensuring that everybody was properly fed in her absence. I did not have to be the one looking for the food or cooking it alone, but I had to get the team of our family to work: the boys to fetch water and firewood and to look after the animals; the girls to harvest the food and cook it.

My father bequeathed us, the Kabushenga family, a legacy of strong core values such as honesty and truthfulness, justice, equality, value for education, and the belief that one must live within their means lest they become thieves. His children were of equal value without distinction because of gender. This was not just a belief; it was put in practice by giving us equal opportunities and access to resources. It is because of his core values that I have been able to live a fulfilled life. In our homestead today is a house my sister and I were allowed to build next door to our brother. We were given access to land for investment according to our means. A highlight of his life shows how one can come from a life of hopelessness and grow into a fulfilled life.

My father, born in a polygamous family in 1919 to a renowned traditional healer who roamed all over Kigezi (now known as Kabale, Rukungiri, and Kanungu District) to heal people was also a risk taker. His father is said to have been rich with herds of cattle and goats, so he was not interested in education, which he saw as a foreign concept brought in by white people to disrupt lives; especially that of my father, who was a herd boy. But my father did not want to be a herd boy the rest of his life. He told us the story of how he took a risk and managed to rise from being a herd boy to becoming a local Sub county chief,[5] one of the best in a team of local magistrates in the District.

As a young herd boy, he used to watch boys of his age pass by in Boy Scout uniforms and wished he could be one of them. One day, while tending the herd and looking enviously at these boys passing by, a truck (lorry) stopped and the driver stepped out and asked him if he wanted to be like the Boy Scouts he was watching passing by. My father answered in the affirmative, and the man told him to jump into the vehicle. Without a second thought, he jumped in and went off, leaving behind the animals he was tending. According to calculations, he was about fifteen years old.

The man was from Buganda but worked in Soroti, Teso District. Soroti is in the eastern region of Uganda, and Kabale is in the western region, approximately 700 kilometres away. In early nineteen hundred, there were no communications for him to tell his parents what had

---

[5] Sub county chief was a governance position introduced in Kigezi by the colonial government. Kigezi and its people managed their affairs through clan heads; a system that was not understood by the colonisers. They saw Kigezi as backward because we had no Kings or chiefs and the attempt to bring Chiefs from the Kingdom of Buganda was resisted. Instead, they introduced a meritocracy system that they used to appoint County, and Sub county chiefs.

happened and where he had gone. When he came back in his early twenties, he found the family had already carried out the death ritual, known locally as "Okumwera" (shaving the head for the dead, as is customary among my Kikiga culture), assuming him to have died. They had to perform rituals to accept him back as a living son.

His abductor had mentored him well. Although today he could be classified as a child trafficker, my father always spoke well of him. While living in Namulonge research station in southern Uganda, my husband and I learned from my father that his mentor came from the same area. We started a search for him. Almost forty years later, we had an opportunity to reconnect my father with his mentor, Mr. Maweno, who had opened doors to great opportunities for my father. As a result of this, my father was the only person in his family with a basic level of education that he came by through sheer determination and willingness to risk his life. It is because of this that he was able to marry my mother, a young woman with some basic education, with whom they lived for more than fifty years.

My father had been given some training as a hospital orderly in Soroti, but his ability to speak English prioritised him for employment by a colonial agricultural officer as an interpreter. But it is his honesty that marked him out for greater things. The test came when he was left in charge by his boss, and found he had to safeguard a Safe full of money that his boss had forgotten to lock when he went on leave. My father camped in the office day and night for a week, guarding the Safe to ensure no one entered the room.

Our father told of his boss's shock when he entered the office and realised he had left the Safe open with all the cash. But his greater, though pleasant, shock was learning that my father had spent a week in the office guarding the Safe. It is this one act of honesty that transformed Mr. Kabushenga's life, and that of his family and relatives forever. He was recommended to the Colonial Governor for promotion to a more responsible job, and that is when he was appointed to be a Chief in Kinkizi District, to a sub county where his father had travelled as a medicine man. Our lives transformed from being a family of peasants, living from hand to mouth with a mother who walked miles to cultivate communal gardens for a livelihood, to a family with the privileges of a Chief's homestead.

My father progressed well in his career and in 1955 was sent to Aberystwyth in Wales to undergo a course in law. A few years later, he was appointed as a Magistrate for the Kinkizi County, a position he served with utmost honesty until his retirement in 1975. During his time as a magistrate my father had one rule that we all knew as children: "Do not receive free gifts." If a person came to visit us with gifts, no matter what type, we were to send them back, unless they were relatives. Anyone else, he told us, would be somebody with a case in his court who was trying to bribe him. Many a goat were sent away in front of us, because he would summon us to tell us why he had sent the man with his goats away.

I remember one incident, when a woman who was married to a minerals prospector visited us in my father's absence and brought with her deliciously cooked food.

Unsuspectingly, we all ate the food, my mother included. When our father came, my mother told him about a visitor we had had during the day and the delicious food she had brought. We saw my father's face change with anger as he asked, "You ate the food? Do you not know that her husband has a case in my court?" Of course, we did not know, and he conceded it was his fault for not telling our mother. I think it is that experience that made him open up to discussing his court cases with us. We never again fell for bribes disguised as cooked food.

This is the background that has defined me. Today, I recognise myself as an uncompromised product of my parents, William and Justine. They taught me the meaning of stewardship and how to be a resourceful leader and manager from a young age. They taught me the value of information, and I am still following their practice; I still listen to BBC programmes, on a real radio, first and last thing in the day.

I learned from them that education transforms lives, and because of that I loved school, I still do, and buried my head in books all the time, because my parents rewarded studying hard. They taught me how to live within my means, and today, to make sure I live within my means, I still carry my snacks to work so I do not have to spend money buying expensive food I may not like. My children find it puzzling that I throw away nothing, until it is unbearably old. I save all the jars, and good plastic bags are stored away even when the opportunity for reuse is not immediately clear. I use my soap until it is no longer big enough to rub between my hands and the toothpaste until the tube proves it has nothing left to squeeze out.

My father had no tolerance for late-comers; he would threaten to leave you, even when you were the sole reason for his taking out the car from the garage. I tell my colleagues and the youth I mentor that if they want to see the monster in me, they should come late for an appointment. I am basically known as a no-fuss person, but I have exceptionally low tolerance for poor performance resulting from low self-exertion, and absolutely zero tolerance for late-comers, thieves, and liars. I too regard an unproductive day as not an option. I learned to love working with women, I believe, because my mother introduced me to working with them at a young age. I saw how much pleasure it gave her to have conversations with women and teach them skills. I went into the work I do today and have done for a lifetime, literally following in my mother's footsteps.

My mother also taught me the value of family and kinship ties; and it pains me that, after she died, there was a rift in the family she tried to keep together. She did not only invest in knowing but also loved and respected her relatives. She made the effort to let us know who our uncles, aunties, and cousins are, no matter how far removed they were. She would constantly want to know when last I talked to her favourite uncle, Mr. Charles Kabuga, who automatically was my grandfather, as she always reminded me. She would call purposely to ask when I last saw Margaret, a daughter of her favourite brother, Mr. John Bikangaga. Margaret and I also became close, and still are, because our parents were. I prefer to be a relatively late riser from bed, but my mother taught me that one has to work a full day, no matter what time they wake up. So I make up by working tirelessly throughout the day, to the discomfort of my colleagues at work sometimes, whose productivity wanes toward the end of the day when mine is peaking.

Today, I stand strong because I watched and learned from my mother, who stood strong in and against patriarchal expectations and norms that were testing her to the limit. I also watch women all over the world standing to the breaking point and still being told to stand up, because their work is not recognised. I am grateful to them all for such an ordinary but rich life in experience and to have had such empowering parents.

CHAPTER TWO

EDUCATION AND CAREER

THROUGHOUT MY LIFE, equality and success at what I do have been two of my life's goals. I did not set out to be a woman getting to the top of the ladder; however, I did set out to create a rewarding, successful life in my endeavours. My story is not just for girls and women; it is just as much for men. Everyone can have their benchmark of success and work hard to achieve it. My benchmark for success is that I finish what I start and enjoy it while doing it. I also believe I am known for doing what I do well; and I am acknowledged as someone who has always worked towards putting girls' and women's rights at centre stage. I have also come to appreciate that life is a gift that comes with both good and tough times, and I have learned to use both experiences positively.

When I was five years old, I was sent to boarding school by my parents, but I was totally unable to cope and was sent back home after the second term of school. Later on, when I asked my mother why she had sent me to boarding school at such a young age, her reasoning at the time was that she wasn't sure whether her husband (my father) would value education for his daughters. So, she took me to boarding school, so that he would have no excuse to keep me home. Of course, her fears were unfounded, because my father turned out to be a proponent of education for both girls and boys, but clearly my mother was already standing up for her girls' right to education.

My recollections of that period are vague and extremely limited, but I remember that I was constantly losing my things like cups, spoons, and even books. It seemed that I was always searching for something in the school compound. Once, I lost my cup, so I could not go to breakfast. A teacher found me looking in the grass and laughed at me, before setting out to help me. That memory stands out clearly in my mind. I also remember I had an exceedingly kind teacher, the founder of the school, Miss Hornby. She would take me to her room and give me special treats because I was so little and fragile. I was in the school for two terms, and I remember her summoning my mother to the school, sitting with us, and saying to her, "Please take your child back. She's too small, too young. She is not coping, and my bananas that I keep especially for her are finished." So, I was sent back home, not with a feeling of shame but of love from both teacher and parent.

As a child, I was always sick and remember spending time in hospital with doctors and my parents hovering over me. When my mother took me away from boarding school, my next place seems to have been a hospital. What I remember from my times in hospital are the kind doctors who would come and see me. They would refer to me as "little girl," because I was also tiny, as well as being young.

I vividly remember the time I woke up to find my mother crying and packing my things, ready to go home. Apparently, I had collapsed into unconsciousness, and she thought I was dead. That is why I see my life as a gift, because I could have died then. I am told the reason I did not die is because the doctor stayed on duty and kept working with me after I weakened; he gave me an injection and continued calling my name until I became conscious again. He did everything he could to ensure that I did not die on his watch. This part of my life story stuck with me, because someone other than my parents cared about me. I was just a patient, but he cared enough to stay at work and nurse me. His caring saved my life, and I was able to go back to school; that has had a profound influence on who I am. With care, you can bring people back to life.

Dr. Kafuko, a man from Busoga in the Eastern part of Uganda, became a permanent friend of my parents in the western part of Uganda. That was possible then. Today, I worry about a country where the new norm is that you live, study, and work only where you were born. It worries me because I see it as a fuel for othering and discrimination.

Another health-related memory that lingers with me is how my mother would detoxify all her children once a year, until we were old enough to refuse. At the end of every year, my mother's sister would arrive for the visit dreaded by all of us; as children, we believed her sole purpose was to torture us with her herbal concoctions. These would be prepared and given to us in millet porridge, because they were bitter beyond description. Within half a day, we would all be sick and weak, throwing up and convinced we were dying. My aunt would then dissect all the products of our vomit, pointing out which one of us had been poisoned and had the most need of detoxifying, then she would give that person a little more. Most times, I was that person. Within a few days, all would be well. My mother and her sister would explain patiently that this process was an immune booster, like the ones given in hospitals against measles. During the COVID-19 pandemic, to which I also became a victim, I thought of her constantly. She would have been a great doctor for the virus, and maybe it was my love of herbal drinks that boosted my immunity and prevented my going into a crisis. Perhaps I got my faith in African herbs from my mother and her sister. My garden today is full of medicinal herbs and the fridge holds herbal concoctions, both bitter and not bitter.

I finally recovered well enough to go back to school and I made the most of the opportunity. Every time I sat in class, I made sure I absorbed everything. I was determined to move to the top of the class and was able to achieve this most of the time. I was also very conscious of the need to pass well, so that I could move to a secondary school level where I did not have to walk to school, come rain or shine.

I got into Junior Secondary School in Kabale, a district town, which was a huge achievement for a village school girl from Kanungu. That year, I was the only student from the whole county to go to what was known in the fifties and early sixties as junior secondary. For the first time, I experienced bullying and, like all bullied people, looked forward to revenge when fresh students came into the school.

But what stands out in my memory from this period is not the harm students caused one another. It is a school rule that made me do something to make me shiver with shame to this day when I think of it. This school had a rule that every student had to come to school with two blankets and a pair of shoes. My father was not poor; both my parents used to wear shoes that they would order in a catalogue from the UK. My father had become a local government chief and could have bought us shoes; but we children never had shoes for the whole of our primary school. As I mentioned earlier, my parents did not want us marked out as different and it made sense. But now, for the first time, I was going have shoes, so the school rule about shoes excited me.

My challenge and source of shame is related to the rule that required students to report to school with two blankets. Kabale, a town in southwest Uganda where I went to Junior Secondary school, was a very cold place in the fifties and sixties, where temperatures would be exceptionally low at night and early morning. When I reported for first term in the junior secondary school, I went with one blanket, and at the end of term, my dormitory teacher warned me that I had to bring a second blanket next term, otherwise I would be sent back home. Already, I was feeling belittled by being the only girl with one blanket. I also knew my parents did not have enough money to buy a second blanket.

I went home for holidays and kept quiet about the rule of two blankets. When time came to go back, I told my parents about the school rule and the threat from the teacher that without that second blanket I could not go back. On the morning of my departure, I went to their bedroom to tell them I could not go without the blanket. I remember being so upset that I cried. My father pulled the blanket from their back and said, "Here is your blanket. Take it, and now you can go back to school."

I have replayed that scene over and over in my head, and the look of love on my parents' face as they took their only blanket and gave it to me—it is one look I can never forget. But I also look back with gratitude that my parents would deprive themselves so I could go school. However, I mention this because this gratitude became another motivation for excelling; I always reminded myself that I took a blanket off my parents' back, so how could I fail them, how could I possibly repay so much unconditional love?

That has been my driving force. I believe, when people love and trust you, when people sacrifice to invest in you, you have a responsibility to deliver.

Education and Insights into Life

Looking back at my education and comparing this with what I hear from girls and young women today, I realise how different our experiences have been and how privileged we were to be educated in violence-free environments. Today, when the government is battling with teachers' battering and sexually molesting girls in school, I look back and am grateful that I spent a life free from abuse in my village school in the fifties, sixties, and even the seventies.

I went to primary school in a religious centre called Nyakatale, in what is now known as Kanungu District. It had a boys' side and a girls' side of the school. The teachers of the boys' school and our teachers would set up competitions for us between the boys and the girls, to test who could write the best English or who could answer the questions better. The competitions were always academic. It was also a competition between the teachers, to see who had the best students, as that would make them the better teacher. That ensured that the teachers were motivated to have the best students, as they wanted to win. The teacher whose students did not get the top position had to buy a gift for the best student. I remember getting a beautiful ink pen from the teacher in the boys' school, because I had scored the best marks in the English competition against the boys in his school.

I was reminded of this during a recent training session (2019) for teachers on women's rights in the northwest of Uganda, where my organisation carries out most of the work of mentoring girls to stay in school. We were advocating against gender violence within the schools. During the training, I listened to teachers talking about educated women in a disparaging manner, making excuses for beating their students, and describing girls as incapable of being top students. I asked teachers what they thought their job was as teachers. The majority answered that they were grooming girls to become good and well-behaved wives. Asked what a good wife was, the description was a replication of patriarchal messaging to women: "Respect and listen to your husband, work hard, and know that your place is subordinate to the husband, who is the head of the household."

What struck me is how different the way teachers of 2019 and my teachers of the 1950s perceived girls. In our case, they saw us as students who could compete academically with the boys in the other schools. Their teaching was not focusing on making us "future good wives," but on making us the best students with high aspirations. It was never who was going to make a good wife out of the girl students, so the competition equalized us with boys. Today, some girls are told they do not have to work hard because they will get married and be well taken care of.

My first granddaughter, one of three, who attended an international school, at seventeen years of age asked me what a feminist is. I was excited about the question and seized the opportunity to lay it out so she had the correct perspective of who a feminist is without the negative branding that comes from inadequate understanding of what feminism really is. I explained that feminists work to make sure women and girls can exercise their agency, have a voice, and enjoy their rights. I explained that feminists have no tolerance for violence against girls and women. I also explained that feminists are usually unpopular, because they refuse to be diminished by some of the social norms that expect women to be dependent on men.

A few weeks later, she told me a boy in her school had asked her why she works so hard, when she is going to marry a rich man who will take care of her. I asked her what her response was.

"I asked him, why would my parents send me to school for me to get married and be taken care of?"

"Welcome to feminism," I responded. Unfortunately, some girls believe in and internalise this disempowering messaging which then guides their behaviour; and then we wonder why so many girls in Uganda drop out of school.[6]

Today, many men, boys, and even women and girls all still see girls through patriarchal eyes. They do not see them as students with rights equal with boys, to finish school and live independent lives. We, the MEMPROW team, are told over and over again by the young women in universities that their parents, relatives, and guardians expect them to have a boyfriend-to-be-husband before they leave university. The impact of this pressure is that many young women at university spend a lot of time cooking for boyfriends and washing their clothes in the hope that they will impress them enough to be a permanent partner. Many times, we ask the question, how many of them graduate as couples and get married; most times the answer is zero, even for those with children from the boyfriends they hoped would marry them. I feel lucky this was not my experience growing up, but perhaps I did not see it because of the kind of nurturing I received from my parents and the great teachers I had.

---

[6] Early marriage and pregnancy are leading contributors to girl child drop out from primary school, National Forum on the State of the Ugandan Child Briefing Note: USAI 2015.

My primary school life was a tough time that I look back at and wonder how I achieved success. Sometimes, I stumbled but was picked up all the time. One example is my last year of primary school, which, in the 1950s, ended at Primary 6. I failed my first primary-leaving examination. At that time, if you failed at that stage, as a girl, you were then married-off by your parents. If you passed, you became a teacher or a nurse or you went to junior secondary for three years, with the outcome of becoming a teacher or a nurse if you did not perform well. Those were the options. If you performed very well, you went to ordinary secondary school, then advanced level, and finally university. This is the dream my parents had for me, especially because my mother had dropped out of school early to get married, according to her culture.

My parents were surprised when I failed, as they thought I was a clever girl. Many times, our environment defines us. A girl in a village school in Kanungu,[7] then as now, stood extraordinarily little chance in examinations set at the district headquarters. When I failed, my parents said, "You know what? You are going to repeat, and you're going to pass." Failure and dropping out of school were not an option. They had a dream, and it helped me pass on my

---

[7] Kanungu is a remote and fertile region of green hills and deep valleys, known for gorillas in Bwindi, impenetrable forest, and for the inferno in 2000, when 700 people perished after being locked inside a church by members of a cult, with the doors and windows nailed shut from the outside. It was then set alight.

second attempt, well enough to go to the only Junior Secondary school in the district.

One other occurrence at the time in my Primary school compelled me to work hard enough to pass. My determination came from a force of an experience that would probably not make sense to the new generations. It stands out for me, though, as one powerful defining moment in my life.

One day, it rained very heavily as we were walking home from school. I have to explain that ours was not a walk but a run to and from school because of the distances we had to cover. People of my generation will recognize this. My brother and I, with several others from our village, used to cover long distances, six miles every day, from home to school and back through very steep hills of Kanungu. Walking would not get you to school on time and arriving late was not tolerated.

On this day, there was a tropical thunderstorm. It rained so hard we had to seek shelter. We found protection in a banana plantation. It rained the whole day and the entire night. We could not complete our journey back home. It was unpleasant, but we decided to take refuge in that banana plantation for the rest of the night, on wet ground, each under a banana leaf. But we kept together, and we were safe. In those days, in our village, the community looked out for students. We knew no one would harm us. Today, more than fifty years later, I remember very clearly sitting in that plantation, cold, wet, and miserable, thinking: "This is not going to happen to me again. I am going to pass and leave this kind of life. It's not going to happen to me again. I want a different life to this."

I passed that examination entrance to Junior Secondary that year. In that year, the headmistress from Kabale Junior Secondary School went around the schools in Kigezi looking for bright children to take to her school. When she came to our school, she was told I was the brightest girl in the school. She picked me as a prospective future student, which motivated me further to work hard. That year, I was the only girl in my primary school who was able to move to the famous Junior Secondary school. This life experience allowed me to change the course of my life; it was the defining moment.

Today, in my training work with girls, I encourage them to flash back and look for a defining moment. Some girls are still stuck in negative defining moments that keep pulling them down. Our role is to guide them, through storytelling, to get out from where they are stuck and move on with their life. Today, when I visit my parents' home, I pass by some of the other girls (now old women) I sat in class with. As I go through that village and see them with faces looking like they have had tough lives, I imagine they are living a life I decided I would not live, as I sat down in the banana plantation on that rainy day in 1958. I had parents who believed in me, parents who really believed in education; but also, it was my determination that moved me away from that life course.

The biggest and most impactful transition in my education life came when I passed my Junior School examinations well enough to get a district scholarship and be admitted into Gayaza High School. Started by missionaries in 1905 to train chiefs' wives, it was the best school in the country in the 1960s and for many years after. My mother, recruited by the missionary Ms. Hornby, was among the first few girls in the forties from Kigezi to attend this school, even though her stay was curtailed by an early marriage she knew nothing about. You can imagine the excitement in my parents' home. My father took me shopping and chose everything carefully, including a nice black brassiere—I wonder how he knew my size. He had instructions from the school informing him I would be met at the bus park on arrival by a teacher from the school, so he did not think he needed to go with me. In those days, you had trust that everything would work well and as planned.

I arrived in Gayaza High School, approximately 400 miles away from my home and parents, full of excitement. The first term of school was a great shock for me in many ways. I was from a village school where one was not marked for their economic class, as I was beginning to see in Gayaza. In my village, you were rich in one thing and poor in another. I also came to appreciate my parents' insistence that we would not have shoes when our peers in our community did not have shoes. They made sure we were not marked, even if we were slightly better off than most people in our community.

At Gayaza, there were many girls whom I came to learn were from "prominent homes of chiefs," as well as daughters of government ministers who were classified as "rich families" and expected preferential treatment. Then there were those who had attended the primary section of

Gayaza. They all acted as if the school belonged to them alone and made those of us from the remote villages of Uganda feel as if we were invaders from outer space. I remember some of them clearly referring to some of us girls as "animals." We were treated as if we knew nothing, and they always talked in the local language, Luganda, as if we were not present.

I still remember the first time I had a shower in a common bathroom; it was a traumatic experience for me. As a young girl from the end of the world, according to how my children used to refer to my home of Kanungu, I was already shy about having a shower in a group of girls I had never met. I survived the shower, but as I was beginning to dress, I picked up the beautiful black brassiere my father had bought. One of the girls stared at me with horror in her eyes and told all the others in her local language I believe because she thought I did not understand what she was saying, "Look at her! She is even wearing a black brassiere. This is a sure sign that she is dirty." My self-esteem and confidence zoomed down. This was compounded by the fact that the same girls were always the first to have their hands up when a teacher asked a question in class. I was sure I was doomed to be the last in a class of these brilliant girls. Sometimes bullies behave and look like they're brilliant, even when they mostly are not. I took the bullying as a challenge to prove myself.

My first break at rebuilding my confidence and regaining self-esteem came at the end of the first term. When that term ended, I was among the top three students. That is when I started gaining some respect from the other girls. The entire year and all the years of my school life at Gayaza, I was within the top five students every term. I worked hard for this. My thought process was that I'd been given this opportunity for a better life by my parents and by the district that was paying my school fees. Mostly, though, I could not mess with the best of the chances given, of being at Gayaza High School from where my mother had been plucked prematurely for marriage. I saw myself following in her footsteps, living her dream. I also felt that a village girl could compete with anybody any time and come out on top.

I finished my advanced level and achieved top marks, which opened up unexpected opportunities for me. At that time in the sixties, if you were one of the top students at Gayaza, they would invite you to stay on as an intern, to work under the mentorship of teachers. But also, it meant you remained actively engaged as you waited to go into university. I was selected together with another girl, Christine Lule (now Kigganda) and we spent 6 months before joining university being mentored into leadership and taking responsibility.

Throughout my life, I have worked hard, not to stand out, but because I feel there are people who sacrificed to get me where I am, and I owe them and myself the respect of doing my very best. I tell my grandchildren, your school life is going to be your best life. You make friends, you read, you learn; you can choose who you are going to be at that moment. If you do not choose right, it can also land you in a different place than where you want to be.

After Gayaza, I went to Makerere University College of East Africa now known as Makerere University. It was the college to be at in the sixties, even when there were other colleges, like Nairobi in Kenya and Dar-es-Salaam in Tanzania. I think university life was my best, although I had thought that my advanced-level period was the best before going to university.

At university, you could argue with professors, unlike in schools, and I loved to argue with them. We had great lecturers like Ali Mazrui, Adam Kuper, Peter Rigby, Raymond Apthorpe, and I was in my element, arguing with them. I had learned the art of arguing in my parents' home with my siblings. We were a family of eleven children, six boys and five girls, so you can imagine how everything called for an argument. Even today, we are known as the Kabushenga (my father's name) family that likes to argue. I usually tell people it comes from knowing who you are and what you want from life. My father and mother would sit and listen and, in the end, give judgement.

I carried this art with me to university, where I always sat in front of the class. In the first year, I was with my brother in the class of sociology, and he preferred to sit right in the back. I remember one time I was having an argument with some of the boys in the front row, who wanted to know why I was in the front row, when most girls preferred to sit at the back. My brother shouted from the back, "You men leave my sister alone!" It was nice having that protection and having him watching out for me, as he had done when we walked those many kilometres during our primary school days.

At university, my favourite place was in the library, because I was in university to get the best out of it. Truth be told, I hated study groups, because most of those who wanted study groups would come without preparation. So, I preferred to study on my own in the library; I had a constant reminder that my parents sent me to school to get the best education. I wasn't going to get it from a nightclub. I was going to get it from the library. University, for me, was a place where I could read anything and everything and then go back and read some more.

My motivation at university also came from my lecturers, who marked me out as a promising student. I had one professor who was always asking questions; and when we were allowed to ask questions, I was always the first to ask them. I began to honestly believe in myself when, at the end of first year, I received recognition and a cash prize as the best female student in the Faculty of Arts and Social Sciences by the University Women's Association.

In my second year, I got further encouragement when one of my professors told me he thought I was brilliant. But to go anywhere further, he said, I would have to get a first-class degree; and that first-class degree would get me into Cambridge University, a place that was a dream to be at. He himself had been at Cambridge and was now teaching Social Anthropology, a subject I loved and enjoyed. That was incentive enough, so I studied hard and I got that first-class degree and went to Cambridge. I give credit for that to Professor Adam Kuper. He took the time and focus to motivate me to do better than perhaps I would have without him making me see the possibilities beyond my dreams. By the time I graduated, I had admission for Newnham College, Cambridge University. I made sure that all my marks were first-class marks, and I was actually the first person to get a first class in Sociology in the Faculty of Social Science at Makerere College, University of East Africa in 1970. It was an exciting time and a great feeling, and I felt I was reaping the rewards of all my hard work.

After I graduated from Makerere, I was taken on as a Graduate Assistant, a position offered to the best students which also implied that you could come back to the faculty as a staff. I went to Cambridge to study Social Anthropology because I knew it would prepare me to be a great teacher. I chose Social Anthropology because I loved learning about other cultures, understanding how they operated, and appreciating the value of culture. My recollection of Cambridge is that it was a lot of hard work and high expectations.

It was certainly a challenge when I first went, studying with many of my classmates, almost all of them younger than me, with English as their first language. Most of those who talked to me wanted to know how I got there and how I thought I would cope. I was the only black girl in the class, and there was an assumption behind the questions that I would have different challenges from them. My confidence began to waver. However, I graduated with distinction in my year; I had been taught well by Adam Kuper and Raymond Apthorpe, my Social Anthropology teachers in Makerere. That was when I knew I needed to specialise in Social Anthropology in my career. Cambridge was a place of great opportunities for studying and travel. This motivated me to work extremely hard during school time so that I could enjoy the holidays. In summer, I indulged in travel to different places in the United Kingdom and Europe. I participated in graduate school meetings at the Graduate Centre, a place where I met a man who was later to become my husband. But I also made friends with students from all over the world, some of whom, like Philomena, became lifelong friends.

When I graduated, the sponsor, the Rockefeller Foundation, offered support for my Ph.D. studies and advised me to stay at Cambridge for the Ph.D. What I didn't mention earlier was that I got the opportunity to go to Cambridge not only because I got a first class and had passed the admission examinations, but the department got me a scholarship. The condition was that I would come back to the department, once I got my degree. When I graduated, I was offered a position of a Research Assistant, so I needed to go back. When the Rockefeller Foundation said they would fund my Ph.D. studies, I was not ready and told them I couldn't accept the offer, as I had a duty to go back to Uganda. This was a decision that I remember clearly did not please the gentleman who had come to talk with me.

I had also agreed with my boyfriend that, when we got back, we would get married. That was another exciting transition stage to look forward to and a reason to return home. I went back to Makerere and moved from Research Fellow to Lecturer. I loved teaching, and I loved teaching in the university. I was teaching the subject of my passion, Social Anthropology, which made me incredibly happy.

My husband and I came back to get married in Uganda, having agreed that a marriage at that time would be a distraction. I was also anxious that he meets my parents first and get to know them. That way, he would be able to understand where I was coming from. Jokingly, I told him I could not marry him in England, away from my home, because my parents did not send me to Cambridge to get married.

Then came the bad years of Idi Amin's rule, when everything was censored, including sometimes what you could or could not say in class. After the exit of Idi Amin in 1979 came several regimes that did not give hope. I began to think of exit options. The decision to go for a Ph.D. was triggered by what may seem like mild incidences by many who have not had the same experiences of the brutal rule of the seventies and eighties in Uganda.

The first trigger I remember was going to a shop to buy toilet paper and bread in Wandegeya, a shopping area close to the university. I walked into the shop and asked the price; when the shopkeeper told me the price, I realised I could not afford to buy both bread and toilet paper at the same time. I started questioning what my situation meant, being a university senior lecturer who could not afford both toilet paper and bread at the same time. I told my husband that life was not possible when you had to choose between buying bread and toilet paper.

I was finally pushed over the edge to go for my Ph.D. by an acute sense of fear for the safety and future of our children. The period after the war ended in 1979, with the departure of Idi Amin, came with unexpected insecurity and a lot of military takeovers of civilians' property and shootings. One particular night in early 1981, a missile shot from the top of the Makerere University Hill landed just outside the block of apartments where the children and I lived. The children and I were trembling as we ducked under my bed.

When my husband came from the research station where he worked and lived during the week, as it was impossible during those days to commute daily, I told him, "I am not staying in this country. We can't live like this." I described the incident of the missile. That same weekend, armed gangs came shooting and stole the motorcycle he had parked outside the compound, along with other vehicles. Again, I said to him we had to find a way to get out of Uganda. We agreed that the time had come, for our safety and the safety of our children. We both agreed to start looking for scholarships to get out of the country. We also agreed that whoever got it first would go and take the children with them, and the other one would stay to make sure we never lost connections with our country. We never thought of a life out of Uganda permanently.

I was quite willing to let him go with the children, if he got acceptance first, even if it meant I had to stay behind. The situation was that dire, but I took comfort in the fact that he was a great father and carer. We applied to different places, and I got accepted to Minnesota University before he did. One of the things he and I agreed on, even back when we met in Cambridge, was that Uganda would always be our country, our home. This is why we agreed that one of us would leave for the safety of the children and

HILDA M. K. TADRIA

one of us would stay in the country. We knew, if we both left, the possibility of never coming back would be great, and we did not want that. We were able to raise enough funds through friends to pay for tickets for the children because, although the scholarship would support the children once we were with them there, it didn't cover the cost of getting them there.

In September 1981, I left alone with the children. I think my experience in Minnesota is the only one I would not want to repeat in my life, because it was an exceedingly difficult time with many challenges for me. When I left Uganda with the children, the oldest was seven and a half years and the youngest was six years. I had never been a single parent. My husband and I had been living together for nine years. We had never separated, except when he or I travelled for a few days. Even as a commuter, he was a great parent.

In Minnesota, I was very cold, alone, and depressed. I remember, during the first winter, walking in the bitter cold and feeling despondent; I remember talking to myself to remind me that I had to maintain my sanity because I had children to care for. My motivation to keep going was because of the children. In addition to this, I had a full schedule of courses, because one of the things I had promised myself was that I would not sit in Minnesota doing my Ph.D. for ten years, like some of the students in my class. Through sheer determination and working long hours, I was able to finish my studies, including one year of field work, within the minimum period of five years.

To say I did all this alone, including all my educational attainments, would be a big lie. For my stay in Minnesota, I had a network of friends that I created. They would come and babysit for me in turns during my examinations. My advisors, Professor Gudeman, Janet Spector, and Susan Geiger, ensured that I met my deadlines by going through my work timely. The university towns of Minnesota and St. Paul had great support systems.

What really helped a lot was the transport system that American schools have for their school children and the university for their students. The bus would arrive at 9 a.m., pick the children up from our doorstep, take them to school, and then drop them back at the end of the day on the doorstep again, where they would walk to after-school care. I had to put them in after-school care because I needed to finish up my studies very fast. This helped me greatly, as I was pressed for time always, pushing constantly to get my work done so we could go back home to Uganda. I started this journey in September 1981, and by 1985, after four years and seven months, I had completed my Ph.D. and was ready for another great journey.

How I Learned to Make my Own Rules

My academic career in Minnesota where I took a combination of Social Anthropology with Women's Studies prepared me for the most exciting journey of my life. It was at this time that I began to realize that in the work I wanted to do, especially if I wanted to continue challenging the patriarchal system, I needed to have a theoretical and ideological understanding of how and why patriarchy works to oppress. This would help to give me depth as to why I and many others were fighting for women's rights.

During this time, I began to contextualise the many fights my mother had had and to understand that they were part of a patriarchal context she was standing up against. I started to understand that, when you break patriarchal norms, the punishment is brutal, especially for women, and why that was so. My mother, for example, felt the brutal nature of patriarchy immediately after 1981, and it still pains me that I did not have clarity of understanding the system to support her enough in her resistance to patriarchy.

I may get the years wrong, but I recall an incident that took place during the elections of 1981, when the now-President Museveni stood and lost the elections, basically because very few people knew him then. After the war of 1979, he had come to Makerere, and I attended the meeting where he addressed students and staff. After he spoke to us, I remember going home and telling my mother that this young man was brilliant. My mother loved discussing politics and was actively engaged in it throughout her life. She was fascinated and asked why I thought he was so accomplished. I narrated his first encounter with us on Makerere campus and an incident with one of the professors, whose name I will not mention because he is no longer alive. This professor had addressed him as Major General Museveni while introducing him. Even as a visitor, Museveni, as he was known then, did not hesitate to tell the professor off for giving him a title he did not have.

My mother decided there and then that she would start supporting Museveni. She even went to rallies campaigning for him in Kanungu, and they remained friends until her death in 2015. My father, however, supported Uganda People's Congress, another party they had both been passionate supporters of since before independence. He did not stop my mother from supporting a party of her choice; he knew my mother too well. He was also an amazingly different kind of man who believed in independent thinking and agency. I know I am where I am today mostly because of that.

Most men and some women from the community did not like the fact of my mother supporting another party and started to come to my father's home, saying his wife had disobeyed and disrespected him as a head of household by supporting Museveni. My father, the amazing man that he was, did not pay attention to them. When Museveni lost the elections, politics and patriarchy merged in the same way that sometimes religions and capitalism merge, to oppress women. These men came to my parents' home threatening to kill my mother. Such was the nature of patriarchal mindsets that they were willing to punish her on behalf of my father, even when he had not asked them to.

My mother had to flee for her safety and went to Kabale, our original birthplace, where she took refuge for a year. She came to me to tell me about it, and although I gave her some support, my regret is that I did not have clarity about the way patriarchy works at that time. Had I known then what I know now about the power of patriarchy on women's lives, I would have supported her better. I did not, and I remember thinking at the time maybe she could have just kept quiet and not gone campaigning, and then none of this would have happened. She would not have had to flee. Today, I realise that is the thought process of the patriarchal mind-set. Keep quiet and things will be okay, but actually they never are. I am glad my mother was not like that; she stood out to do what she thought was best for her, irrespective of the consequences.

Whilst she was away, patriarchy went to work again, trying to fix my father's life by getting him another wife. They brought one woman after another, all of whom he rejected. My mother tells me, when she went back, my father told her about the men who would bring the numerous girls for my father to marry. My father one day asked these people who were persistent in trying to get him a wife, "Do you know my wife, Justine?" When they said yes, he then asked, "Do you think these little girls you have been bringing for me can fill Justine's place? If you know my wife, you know that no one can fill her place." They finally gave up on him, and my mother returned to her matrimonial home, and my parents lived happily after that for many years.

I only came to understood what was happening to my mother in her community when I took a course in women's studies for my Ph.D. at Minnesota University. For me, that was the most enriching course, because I started to understand how patriarchy works as a system of rules and practices, privileges, and power, as well as through subordination and control. Today, it is this clarity of mind that has defined my feminist ideology, and this is what guides the work of my organization, MEMPROW, as well as my advocacy and activism for women's rights. We train the girls, boys, and communities we work with to understand how this system works.

You need to understand the story behind the story of what you see, because then you can fight back better. Had I known that the story behind the story of men chasing away my mother was because she rebelled against the patriarchal system, I would have supported her better in challenging the system more. Whilst I had studied Social Anthropology, I had never understood the underlying power of patriarchy and how it determines what we do, what we say, even what we eat. In the community where we, at MEMPROW, do our work, for example, many women still do not eat chicken, because it is for the men; women eating it is regarded as disrespecting men.

Investing in education up to my Ph.D. had benefits other than giving me the courage to set my own rules; it opened new opportunities for me. My life was transformed because of this investment. While I was in Minnesota, finalising the first part of my Ph.D. studies in 1983, I was invited for the first time to present a paper at a conference on women in development that was being held by an organisation now known as the Association for Women's Rights in Development (AWID). It is a global feminist membership and movement-support organisation. I began to understand the power of my education and knowledge. Since then, I have used it to break barriers set by sexism to discriminate women and girls using patriarchy norms.

I went back to Makerere in May 1985, a period I remember very well, when I took up my position as Senior Lecturer. I remember that period well, because it is the time when I became aware of the sexism institutionalised in norms and practices at the University, in spite of the fact that I had experienced sexism in different forms before my study in Minnesota. An interesting example of this is that, when I was preparing to go for my Ph.D., my Faculty Dean, who was also my boss, advised me not to go for further studies. When I had gone to his office to bid him farewell, he asked me if my husband had a Ph.D. When I told him he did not, my dean looked at me with great sympathy and, in a serious tone, said, "Do not go. You will be emasculating your husband." I had experienced unconscious sexism and I did not think twice about it because I did not recognise it for what it was.

It was not until after my course in women's studies that I understood the role my Dean was trying to play. Instead of encouraging me, his employee, to improve myself and serve the institution better, he was encouraging me to stay and serve my husband better. When I came back five years later to the same faculty, I remember this period as one of fighting back, because the Department of Sociology was full of men. I found myself the only female member of professional staff.

I came back to find a vacancy for an Associate Professorship advertised. The only qualification needed to apply for it was a Ph.D. and a few years' experience, both of which I had. I went to my head of department and told him I was going to apply for this job and asked if I would have his support. He said he was not going to recommend me, because he was planning to propose a male colleague whom I knew did not even have his Ph.D. I informed my head of department that I would apply anyway, and he was welcome to support the male colleague.

I now understood how the patriarchal mind-set worked, and I was willing and ready to stand up to it, whereas before I would have said, "Okay, I will wait." I got the appointment to Associate Professor, but this became a permanent reminder to me of what happens to women when the system weighs so heavily on us that we cannot stand up for our rights.

I remember a time in 1973 when I failed to stand up for myself because I did not understand how patriarchy makes us collude to take away our choices. I had just gotten married in December 1972. A few months later, I received a letter from the University Secretary threatening to withdraw my salary the following month. My crime was very clearly spelt out:

Dear Miss Kabushenga,

We understand you recently got married; however, you are still using your maiden name. If you do not change your name, you will not receive your salary.

My husband and I had already agreed that there was no need to change my name to his. But my employer took on the role of making sure the patriarchal norm of assuming a husband's name became a practice in my home. In 1972, the comprehension of my oppression was very low, and I rushed to change my name. My personal identity was obliterated forever, without a single fight from me. At the time, I did give in to patriarchal pressure to change my name, because I did not know then what I know now. The fear of having no salary took priority; as a young married woman, it was a greater threat than the need to fight for my identity. Little did I know that by accepting the name change I, too, was conforming to the principles of patriarchy brought into formal institutions. Interestingly, 6 months later, I received another later from the same official.

Dear Mrs. Tadria,

We notice that you have been working in the country without a work permit. Should you fail to regularise your status, you will be prosecuted.

I picked up the telephone and called the University Secretary who had signed the later. I introduced myself and explained why I was calling him. "You sound Ugandan," he said. "I am Ugandan," I responded. "Forget the letter," he said, end of story. He had no idea how all these incidences played on my mind.

At the time, I could not understand why my employers were so keen to make me change my name, forcing me into an identity change that I had not planned. Not until later did I understand how the power of patriarchy operates. Subsequently, while studying for my doctorate in Social Anthropology and women's studies, I finally got answers to my questions. I began to appreciate that the identities imposed on me at different stages of my life came from an underlying common patriarchal view, reinforced by colonial Christianity, that women must live under the identity of a man, preferably their father, husband, or brother. Yet, in the Bakinga traditional culture where I was born, wives and children never took the names of the husband and father. This is an important example of how colonial thinking about women transformed gender relations in my culture. With this came the change in gender roles, where the man became the head of household simply because he was the one given opportunity to work for monetary rewards.

During my field research of my Ph.D. in Sseguku and Ndejje, I learned from both the men and women that the dichotomy between men's crops as cash crops and women's crops as food crops was a false dichotomy imposed during colonial times in order to bring men into the cash economy. Before that, both men and women were involved in growing food crops. A Muganda man who did not have a proper Lusuku (banana plantation) from which to feed his family was viewed as not a responsible man.

This restructuring of the household economy also restructured gender relations and entrenched the subordination of women, who in reality grew crops that men were selling. I also learned that, because the cash earned from the external manual labour men were engaged in was never enough, women's labour in food and cash cropping were subsidising the capitalist colonial economy. In this system, the employer could afford to pay the male labourer less than his market value.

Steve Gudeman, whose economic anthropology guided my thinking in my field study, discusses what happens when labourers are drawn from the subsistence sector,[8] in "Changing Economic and Gender Patterns among the Peasants of Ndejje and Sseguki in Uganda." I found that the subsistence economy was undermined by the capitalist economy through the diversion of both its natural resources and labour. But more, it introduced a hierarchy of gender roles, where women were given a subordinate, supportive role.

My findings agreed with Gudeman's concept of capitalist exploitation when I found a subsistence economy (food crops) was giving support to the capitalist economy when those who were taken out were paid low wages for production in the subsistence sector. Several writers have attributed the deterioration of the position of women compared to men to the inequalities established and entrenched within a capitalist economy. In my research, I found that the complementary economic relations and roles were undermined as women's work became undervalued, while men laid claim to their crops for cash. Unlike in the past, when both women and men had a claim to the household produce. In Uganda, this is how the different gender roles and differential treatment of a male as a cash owner (more status) was entrenched as an operating principle in relations between women and men.

In her recently published book, Professor Sylvia Tamale of the Law School in Makerere University, with her

---

[8] Reference: "Changing Economic and Gender Patterns among the Peasants of Ndejje and Sseguki in Uganda: a Thesis submitted to the faculty of University of Minnesota ,"1985.

powerful analysis, exposes the clear impacts of colonialism that supports my findings in the field.

> *Significantly, colonial processes restructured hierarchical power relations based on gender, class, education, sexuality, etc. The dichotomous understanding of gender in terms of polarized, hierarchized identities (i.e., masculinity vs femininity) was imposed on the colonized through processes of colonialism. To put it differently, the political economy of gender relations between African women and men was totally altered by colonialism, engendering new structural drivers of inequities.*[9]

There are other ways in which colonialism, in partnership with religion, transformed cultural norms that had long been practiced and were not harmful to the society. The practice ensured that everyone had their identity. In traditional Bakiga culture, homesteads were known by the women's names, perhaps so that women in

---

Sylvia Tamale. *Decolonisation and Afro-Feminism*. Draja Press, 2020. p.49.

Paul Tiyambe Zeleza, Professor of the Humanities and Social Sciences and Vice Chancellor, United States International University-Africa, Nairobi, Kenya, describes this book aptly in the review when he says, "In this extraordinary and erudite book, Sylvia Tamale, the distinguished Ugandan scholar and public intellectual, brilliantly dissects and demolishes the dangerous tropes of coloniality that distort our understanding of African societies, cultures, bodies, institutions, experiences, social relations, and realities. She unsparingly and compellingly advances the analytical power and emancipatory possibilities of decolonial feminism."

polygamous marriages would not lose their identities. In this culture, the title "Nyineka," which is given to a head of the household (male) among Bakiga, when translated into English actually means "mother of the home." In addition, a woman received a new and different name from her husband by the family she married into, usually after a period of observing her behaviour, so her new name reflected her character and position rather than marking her as property belonging to her husband. It leaves a question as to when the men became the heads of household among Bakiga and the link to imposition of foreign patriarchal norms.

My loss of identity in 1973 was a repeat of my experience in 1959, when I first lost an identity while registering on for Junior School. At the registration point, a white missionary teacher asked for my name. When I told her, she hesitated before writing it on the form and asked me, "Is this your father's name?" To which I said, "It is my name." Her dismissive answer was, "No, that is your pagan name. I want your father's name," which she then proceeded to record instead of my name. Doing a Women Studies for my Ph.D. I finally understand why my personal name, given at birth by my parents, was classified as a pagan name, while my father's name given to *him* at birth was not classified as pagan. He was seen as the patriarch whose identity defined me.

My maternal grandmother was an example of the harmful effects of the colonial mentality mixed with Christianity. A woman of small stature but a hard worker, she had her life disrupted when her husband, a polygamist, became baptised into the Christian religion. "The European missionaries condemned polygamy and some other African culture entirely."[10] Her husband, a local chief at the time, was advised to send away all his wives except the first wife, as a confirmation that he was a true convert. But this is the irony of Christianity, a supposedly caring religion that ended up affecting my mother and her mother in many detrimental ways. My grandmother was uprooted from a place she had known for many years as home. She had been a child bride, but she was sent away, leaving her two daughters behind, my mother being one of them. She remarried, and I spent many happy times in her new home. My regret today is that I was not wise enough to ask her about her life (the drama and the trauma it must have caused her), although we had many other discussions most of them focusing on her need to know when I was going to get married, seeing as I was spending too much time in school.

My Career

Very often, young people ask me whether they should pursue Ph.D. studies to "waste" a few more years. I never

---

[10] *Global Journal of Arts Humanities and Social Sciences,* Vol. 4, No.10, pp.18-28, October 2016. Published by European Centre for Research Training and Development UK (www.eajournals.org) 18 ISSN: 2052-6350(Print), 2052-6369(Online) "Polygamy and Christianity in Africa." T A Falaye, Ph.D. Department of Religious Studies Olabisi Onabanjo University, Ago-Iwoye Ogun State, Nigeria.

tell them whether it would be good for them or not, but I tell them that, in my case, getting a Ph.D. opened doors, many of which I was not even knocking at.

My first international job was presented to me on a platter a few months after my return from Minnesota to Uganda. I was invited to serve as Facilitator at the Women in Development regional workshop at the Eastern and African Management Institute in Arusha, Tanzania. Although it was my first time doing that kind of work, I was confident I had adequate knowledge to successfully undertake the job. After all, I had just completed a PhD. in Women Studies.

I had been a university lecturer but never a facilitator, a role that calls for a different approach to sharing knowledge. I consulted my new networks to get a proper understanding of what it entailed and then accepted the week-long assignment without fear. After the week, when I was getting ready to leave, Misrak Elias, who had invited me to the Institute, asked if I would like to interview for a consultancy vacancy. I did not hesitate to accept the invitation for the interview, and before I left, I was told I was the best candidate for the job. This was an exciting moment in my transition. I had come there as a temporary facilitator, invited by a person I had never met, and now I was going back as a full-time consultant in the renowned and highly respected Management Training Institute. Doors were opening unexpectedly.

I went back to Uganda and had a discussion with my husband. We had been living apart for almost all the five years while I was away doing my Ph.D. During the last two years of my studies, he had lived alone with the children, so I could focus on writing my thesis. I had doubts about whether I should go away again so soon. This was towards end of 1985, still a very turbulent period in Uganda, with fears of another military takeover, something we had to consider when deciding our next steps.

My husband said, "If anything happens here, you and the children need an exit. So, don't say no." Indeed, we left in the first week of January, and a new military government entered Kampala on 26 January 1986. Having a vision of a safe future for our children guided our decision-making processes in tough times and saved us many difficulties.

There was also another reason for hesitating before accepting the job. When I returned in 1985, I founded an organisation called Action for Development. This organisation was started because I wanted to contribute to the women's movement following the Third World Conference on Women that took place in July 1985. I had missed the opportunity to attend this conference because, in those days, one needed permission to travel out of the country. If you were not affiliated to the then-ruling party, you could be denied permission.

Sometimes I feel we have gone full circle, when I listen to our leaders talking about which area does or does not deserve government development projects. Although my father had been a strong subscriber to the party UPC, I had no affiliation to them. I believe my supervisors at University were not sure whether they would be penalised for giving me clearance, even though at that time academic freedom meant that you could attend conferences, so they took a cop-out option. The Vice Chancellor asked me to produce clearance from the then-National Women's Organisation, a government structure dancing to the ruling party tune. It seems in this area, nothing has changed much as privileges still come to those who dance the party tune best even in government programmes.

When I missed this conference, one that every woman activist looked forward to and strived to attend, I decided to turn my great disappointment and feminist rage into positive energy. Civil society organising had collapsed. I felt a strong urge to revive civil society activism that would stand up for women's rights and choices. At that time, in September 1985, an idea became reality, and Action for Development, an organisation created to fill a gap and meet the need of advocating for women's rights, was formally launched.

Several women became founding members. The original women I brought on board were my colleagues at Makerere University: Ms. Joy Kwesiga, now Professor and Chancellor of Kabale University; and Professor Ruth Mukama, retired from Makerere and now in Kabale University. We had our first meeting where I tabled my idea which they bought into. We agreed that we needed to situate it into the Global women's agenda (the Nairobi Forward Looking strategies) that had been developed to guide gender equality work. We recognised a need to invite someone who had attended the conference.

Dr. Maxine Ankrah, now retired lecturer from Makerere University came to mind and we invited her to the next meeting. When I shared my possibility of a new job and my reluctance to take it because of ACFODE they encouraged me to take up the opportunity, promising they would make sure the organisation does not close because of my absence. Maxine would take over from me as the next Chair of ACFODE. The team was committed to the organisation, and they held it. It still stands today, holding its own.

The decision to leave Makerere University, an institution I had studied at and that had nurtured my career, was a difficult one to make. I compared the opportunity for a great and exciting job in a safe environment for our children with a looming war and decided to ask for leave of absence to join the Eastern and Southern African Institute. My job was to bring the ideas of gender and development into the work of managers, both men and women within the Eastern and Southern African region. I was given one year's leave, but before it was over, I received a letter from the Vice Chancellor's office telling me that I had fled from duty and was therefore fired from my position. I thought about challenging this decision of dismissal without warning, especially when I had been given permission. I found myself asking, would they have dealt with a male senior member of staff in the same manner? But I decided I would not challenge it, because I was in a good place, doing work I loved. I decided to cut my ties with them. This is a decision I have never regretted.

The work at the Institute was exciting on one hand and depressing on the other. I began to encounter stories of women experiencing oppression and exclusion as well as abuse of power because of patriarchy in the workplace; women with no awareness of the source of their oppression.

Women in management who talked about the challenges of balancing work, family, and social expectations. But it was exciting to reveal the power of patriarchy and see both attitude and behavioural changes in my follow-up visits.

I recall an example of one female manager who shared her story of how she would wake up at 5 a.m. to polish the floors of her house every day before going to work, because she thought her husband liked floors polished by her. She shared with me her concerns about her lack of energy and tiredness in the workplace. At the time she came to the training, she was feeling she was not delivering on the workplace expectations and feared this would lead to her being replaced. She was trying to be Wonder Woman, even when she could have paid for cleaning services.

When we discussed how patriarchy works in a woman's life and especially in marriage, she realised she was trying to fit in the patriarchal normative framework of expectations for a wife. When I met her years later, she told me she was a better manager and secure at her workplace because she changed her strategies and stood up against the unrealistic expectations of patriarchy. But most importantly, she and her husband finally recognised that a floor polished by somebody else was as good as the one polished by his wife.

I was able to change lives because I had new knowledge from my further education. In the early eighties, thinking about integrating women's issues and concerns into the development agenda was just beginning, and there were questions as to whether equality would ever be achievable. Women managers would come into training with questions about whether it was possible to be equal to their husbands or their male colleagues. Many of them were their own censors; quoting the Bible that is clear about women's submission to men. These women had entered into male-dominated workplaces with poor self-worth and low self-esteem and yet hoped for equal treatment.

My career at ESAMI came with many opportunities to serve the whole of Eastern and Southern Africa, a region that covered nine countries at the time. I had the fortuitous opportunity to visit the United Artists for Africa in California, an organisation that provided what in those days was a huge grant to support our women in development. I still maintain this link, created in the eighties.

I also had an opportunity to visit the United Nations International Research and Training Institute for the Advancement of Women (UN-INSTRAW), which had been created as a result of the recommendation of the First World Conference on Women in 1975, to be dedicated to the advancement of women. The visit to UN-INSTRAW, which was based in Santo Domingo, Dominican Republic, stands out for both good and bad memories. The good memories are the beauty of the country and hospitality of its people. It is also at UN-INSTRAW that I met Grace Bediako, a young woman from Ghana and a brilliant statistician, who became a valued resource person in training women in statistics at ESAMI.

The nasty experience that remains vivid even today was the humiliation I was subjected to on my return, when I was apprehended in transit at JFK airport and put under police custody. My passport was taken away, and I was given a guard the entire period until it was boarding time. I could not even go to the bathroom without permission or an escort. I no longer had a name, and I was referred to as a TRAW. I still have no clue what that meant. I had gone through the same airport to Santo Domingo without trouble, but on return, traveling on the same passport, through the same airport, I became a criminal. I remember the African-American policewoman who drove me putting me in the back seat of the police car next to her clothing and her giving me a stern warning not to touch her clothes.

I continued to be humiliated when we reached my boarding gate, with me chained to her as she handed my passport to people at the gate and adding the explanation that I was a TRAW. I was given my passport back one hour after take-off. I did not understand the logic of not being given my passport until an hour later, when clearly there were no opportunities for jumping out of the aeroplane. But now finally, in hindsight, especially since the Black Lives Matter campaign, I have a new understanding of "unconscious institutionalised racism" and sexism and how everyone colludes, to maintain the system.

After a few years living in Arusha, in 1990, I was given an opportunity to move to Harare in Zimbabwe as the Institute's Ambassador. This was a fulfilment of an unspoken dream: to live in Zimbabwe, a country in whose struggle for independence I had remotely participated in through protest walks while a student in Makerere in the 1960s. I had first visited Harare in 1987 and admired the country that had just gained independence in 1980. It was highly organised and the systems worked. I remember going from office to office and being struck by how young and confident all the managers who occupied offices of high responsibility were.

Representing the Eastern and Southern Institute came with many privileges. But after two years, I began to feel that I was losing track of my core life's goal: fighting for gender justice and working directly with women did not fit in well with government diplomacy and Institutional representation.

I began to seek out new opportunities. In January 1990, I found it in the African Capacity Building Foundation (ACBF), where I worked for only two years then decided to retire, even when it was not clear where I would go. The ACBF was set up with great intentions to serve as a Specialized Agency for Capacity Development in Institutions. But for years, the leadership seemed to be more interested in serving their own interests.

Having worked at ESAMI, I saw regional and national training institutions as possible great partners in capacity building, but the idea did not seem to be welcome in my new work place. At ACBF, I was the only female professional and a lonely voice for gender justice and equality. Our job was to evaluate and recommend projects for funding, but gender equality was not on the agenda of the people who were approving the grants. I began to feel a sense of purposelessness.

Ironically, my final push to move out of ACBF came through an opportunity to act as Executive Director for a few weeks. During the absence of the Executive Director, his stepdaughter came to Zimbabwe for her holiday and requested that I write a letter authorising her to stay at the Sheraton Harare on ACBF's budget. I refused, explaining that my instructions did not include allocating budgets to the family members of the Executive Director. I explained I could request the hotel give her a room pending the return of the father, who would meet the costs. I felt that a woman over twenty years of age was perfectly capable of taking care of herself in her parents' home, which was already being paid for by the organisation and had full security and a team of housekeepers.

When the Executive Director, the stepfather, came back to the office, it was clear through his freezing looks and attempts to exclude me from office work that he was not happy with what I had done. I still had a few months to complete my contract, but I gathered my courage to meet with him and tell him I did not want my contract renewed. I explained to him that at ACBF I was losing my professional skills and was distracting myself from my passion. I believe he was relieved to hear that, and I left at the end of my first contract.

I went back to Uganda in 1994, nine years after I had left the country. That year, my husband retired from formal employment. We were both unemployed, but we quickly set up a consultancy firm, HILCON, named for Hilda and Constantine. My reputation for working for women's right and development had been well established, and consultancies came fast and easy.

We committed to high professional standards. One way of ensuring this was that we made a commitment to take on only one consultancy at a time, as this would lead to uncompromising quality. Most work that came in required gender policy planning and training, so our roles were well defined. He became the chief administrator and editor of my work, a role that fitted him well because he was a meticulous writer. We did this for four years, and we were able to generate enough income to give quality education to our children and support our parents until another great opportunity came along.

My career of ten years at the United Nation's Economic Commission (UNECA) came about totally unexpectedly while on a stopover in Addis Ababa, on my way to West Africa. I decided to make a call on an old friend to say hello and then learned from him that the Commission was seeking to recruit an experienced gender specialist. He assured me I had the necessary credentials.

The following day, I went in to get the job description and application forms from the Human Resources Department. The deadline for submission was about to expire, so I decided to fill in the form and leave it with the official. After handing it to him, he studied it with a sceptical look. The job advertised was a senior position, and it is what I responded to. After a short pause, he looked at me and advised me to apply for a lower level, because the senior position required clearance from the United Nations headquarters, adding that it would not be easy to get clearance for me. Always alert to sexism, I sensed a patriarchal mind-set; I asked myself if he would have said this to a male applicant. I decided to apply for the advertised position nevertheless, informing the official that if New York did not approve, I would be fine continuing with what I was doing. Six months later, I was told I had the job and packed my bags, leaving my husband once again to hold the fort in Uganda.

My job title at the UNECA was as Economic Adviser for women in Africa. This gave me opportunity to travel to almost all African countries, providing gender training service, supporting development of gender policies, and designing gender-sensitive development plans. The ten years of my last career, which marked the end of formal employment, were a fulfilment of all my dreams.

At the UNECA, I was also given an opportunity to be part of the team working on a special HIV/AIDS project that expanded my awareness of the impacts of the disease. I came across child heads of household doing their best to keep things together. I visited a girl of thirteen years in Rakai in Uganda which was the epicentre of HIV/AIDS. She was heading a home of four siblings and a fifth one she had adopted because this child had also lost all her parents and no one had come forward to claim her. I sat with this child heading a household without bitterness and marvelled at her capacity to give, even when she had almost nothing. She told me how she got up early to prepare her siblings for school and then came back to work in the garden. I asked her how she knew it was time to get up. She said, "I hear the birds singing and know it is time to get up." This profound wisdom from a child brought tears to my eyes, and the memory still lives with me.

MEMPROW is born

At the UNECA, I was also given the responsibility of receiving and analysing the country reports from all the ministries in charge of women's affairs and gender equality in Africa and summarising the common issues for discussion in the region. Over the years, I was struck by the commonality of issues reported by the African countries: increased domestic violence; excessive school dropout of girls; teenage pregnancy; and young women's disinterest in joining women's activism against gender-based discrimination and violence. It is during this period I began to think of what I could do to change this situation.

During the same period, I went to Uganda on leave and one day picked up an article in the New Vision, one of the national newspapers, describing results of a research Makerere University had undertaken on how female students set priorities at university. The researcher had provided options of aspirations from which the students were asked to select what they wanted most, which included owning a smart phone, a car, a husband, and passing well. I was stunned by the results, which showed the new norms in aspirations of university-going students. Most girls in university had ranked "passing examinations well" at the bottom of their aspirations. I remember my sense of disbelief and rage. I asked myself, "Who goes to university and passing well is not their first aspiration?" This was five years before my retirement, but it was the real trigger for starting the Mentoring and Empowerment Programme for Young Women (MEMPROW).

By the time I retired from the UNECA in 2017, my idea was fully evolved, with a promise of seed money to start the organisation from a personal friend. When I returned home to Uganda, I wasted no time. I decided to visit schools and universities to understand what the problem behind low aspirations, poor performance, and school dropouts was. From the university girls, I learned that the pressure to get a husband before graduating, powerfully influenced the choices they made.

In Makerere University, young women talked of the pressure to minimise their academic efforts so that boys would not think they were too clever, as a clever girl was not a desirable wife. In Kampala University, the girls talked of the pressure to maintain their relationships by working as maids for the boyfriends. They gave examples of girls who stayed in their rooms to cook, on orders from the boyfriend, even when they had a class to go to, for fear they would lose the boyfriend. The boys would promise to bring back notes to them. I found it mindboggling that a person will depend on the brains of a boyfriend instead of going to class to learn for herself. But such is the power of patriarchy, I reminded myself.

In the schools I visited, I learnt from the girls that sexual violence and a patriarchal mind-set from the teachers contributed greatly to school dropout rates. Today, the work I and my team at MEMPROW do, mentoring girls and young women, is meaningful because it is relevant to the issues they battle with in a patriarchal setting, whether in their homes, at work, or in the institutions of learning.

MEMPROW empowers them with life skills so they can stand up for their rights.

CHAPTER THREE

DEFYING PATRIARCHAL NORMS AND SURVIVING LIFE CHALLENGES

WHEN YOU WORK WITH the younger generation of girls and women, you begin to understand and appreciate the biases and power of patriarchy over their lives even more. The patriarchal biases and stereotypes are held by both women and men in Uganda. Unless you are a feminist, your basic social, political, economic, and political thinking is within the framework of patriarchal mind-set and norms.

In the Ugandan context, for example, we have all internalised the message that a male is the head of household and therefore entitled to the privileges of service from, and authority over, women even at an early age. When I understood the power of patriarchy over my life and that of other women and girls, I set a life agenda of change, focusing on defying patriarchy. I realised that feminist consciousness is not enough; one has to speak out and fight back all the time in every circumstance in order to change the patriarchal normative framework; otherwise, if you snooze you lose the fight. Today, this is my feminist agenda: defying patriarchy.

There are many myths about the appearance and actions of a feminist. During a training session of young women lawyers, I was amused when they expressed shock that well-groomed young women were calling themselves feminists. I have been told that feminists cannot be Christians. In a conversation with some of my male friends, one of them made a sexist remark. I reminded him that I was not happy with the remark and asked him to withdraw it and apologise. He looked at me with incredulity and said, "But Dr. Tadria, you are not a feminist. You are not an angry person like those feminists. You are actually a nice person."

I am definitely a feminist, no ifs, and, or buts about it, according to the African Women's Charter on true feminism. And I also try to be a nice person. But am I an angry feminist? Yes. I tell everybody I am a permanently enraged feminist. I am enraged about the rape of babies, girls, and women. I am enraged that girls do not go to school and those who do are bartered, so their parents, whose responsibility is to look after and educate them, use their education to be able to charge a few more cows in bride wealth.

It makes me angry when women who have lived with educated husbands for a lifetime tell me their brothers-in-law are the administrators of their property, when they themselves are totally capable of looking after the properties they have worked for. I get angry when total strangers stop me on the street to ask me why I cut my hair, when the Bible says it is my crowning glory as a woman. How can hair be my crowning glory? I get enraged because I know they are judging me through patriarchal lenses. I am angry when young women are told they cannot do engineering because they are women, and that no man marries a woman engineer. Similarly, I found it totally annoying when outsiders, using patriarchal mind-sets of male dominance, found it necessary to tell my husband how to make decisions in our affairs.

In 1993, while living in Zimbabwe, a very close family friend passed away in Uganda. When I came for the funeral, I was shocked to learn that his wife was worried about the future for her and the children. Her husband had left no written Will, and she was worried that they would be disinherited by his relatives. My husband and I decided there and then that I should not go back until we had written our Will. We picked a lawyer friend who we thought knew us well and who understood we did not live within the standard prescribed patriarchal norms. After discussing what we wanted in our Will, he told us to go and come back for the document the following day.

We were in his office promptly the following day. When he called us into his office, we noticed there was no document at his desk. My husband and I looked at each other but none of us spoke.

The lawyer started humming and humphing. "*Ahhhh*, I am afraid I did not write the Will." We looked at each other again. "I did not write because I think you are misguided. You are leaving your property equally to your daughter and your son. What if your daughter gets married and dies? Your property will go to another man."

This time we did not look at each other, and we did not say anything. I believe we were each dealing with our shock, and I with my feminist rage.

Sensing disagreement he added, "Unless that is what you want."

This is how unconscious sexism bred by patriarchy works, and if we were equally unconscious, maybe we would have fallen for it. But we quickly responded in unison, "That is what we want."

My husband then added, "What if we left everything to our son? What if he died and his wife remarried? The property would go to another man."

The lawyer, again sensing defeat, replied, "Okay, if that is what you want."

The following day when we collected the documents, we made sure to read them carefully before we left. What I learned from this incident is the value of travelling a feminist journey with my husband and a mutual focus on equal rights for our children.

I often think about this incident and how a total stranger could think to disinherit our daughter just because she is a girl. We had sat with him, we had told him what we wanted, but it did not make sense to him. He was paralysed out of action, but he is not alone in the thinking that girls are entitled to less than the boys. This is how the patriarchal norms work on the minds of those who are unconscious of their negative impacts. It makes you either act or harm others or you are paralysed into inaction. Either way, you will do harm.

I see so many widows struggling to get letters of administration and access to resources they worked for, simply because we (especially men) are afraid to say in writing what should happen when we die; or maybe because we think someone will take charge of the mess we have left behind.

But sometimes, I do have a few laughs. For example, my husband and I sometimes had our titles reversed, after introducing ourselves to people we were meeting for the first time. Immediately after introductions, "I am Dr. Hilda Tadria" and my husband said he is Mr. Tadria, he would be addressed as Dr. Tadria and I, as Mrs. Tadria. Feminist sympathiser that he was, he would immediately correct whoever had had the momentary memory loss, saying, "My wife is Dr. Tadria, not me." I would look at the shock on their faces and laugh. When there is no harm done, one can afford to laugh at the patriarchal mind-set.

Translating Feminist Rage into Positive Action.

As a feminist working to transform negative patriarchal norms, mind-set, and practices, I have learnt to use my feminist rage constructively. It is my feminist rage and the need to fight for equality that gave birth to Action for Development.

This is an organisation I started in September 1985, after I was refused permission to attend the meeting in Nairobi for Forward-looking Strategies for the Advancement of Women in Nairobi, Kenya, 15-26 July 1985. It was my rage against sexual violence and gender discrimination that pushed me to invest my retirement time into starting MEMPROW, an organisation that is mentoring girls so they can stay in school and lead independent lives, even if it is one girl at a time.

Similarly, when I attended the African Regional Conference on Women in Dakar, Senegal, in 1994, which was the preparatory meeting for the Beijing conference on women, I was enraged that women did not have enough resources to organise properly for an effective meeting. It is this which triggered the establishment of the African Women's Development Fund that I co-founded with two African women, Olabisi Adelelye-Fayemi from Nigeria and Joana Foster (RIP) from Ghana.

The African Women's Development Fund (AWDF) is the first Pan-African foundation started by African women to support the realisation and fulfilment of African women's rights through funding of autonomous women's organisations on the continent. The AWDF vision is to have a world where all African women live in peace, with dignity and justice, and where there is equality and respect for women's rights. Throughout my life, I have learnt that I need to build a movement of like-minded people to transform the negative social norms and mind-sets.

In my family life, it is this permanent rage, carefully used, that guided the way I parented our children, both those to whom I gave birth and those I looked after when they lost their father, my younger brother. So, I apologise to them, if they felt my uncompromising value system was an oppression for them. But perhaps my biggest apology is to our daughter, Vanessa, and son, Patrice, because they constantly experienced my feminist rage. Perhaps I was an embarrassment sometimes as I never let a sexist remark go unchallenged.

My daughter did a degree in civil engineering at Loughborough University and has not stopped telling people that she did engineering for her mum. Vanessa was a top student in sciences and mathematics throughout school, as was her brother, Patrice. While at one of the best schools in Southern Africa, Waterford Khamtlaba, where she did her baccalaureate, she was constantly mocked for being the only girl in a class of higher mathematics, allegedly meant for boys only.

She did not quit; but when, after school, she said she wanted to do a business degree, my automatic response was, "No, you cannot. You are supposed to be a scientist." Guided (or misguided) by my feminist fighting spirit, I resisted my daughter dropping sciences in higher education, like many young girls do in Uganda. I needed to make sure that change started in my own house. All my daughter wanted was a career in the economic sector, but she agreed to do civil engineering. She went on to do a master's in information technology at the same university, and a master's in business administration (MBA) at the London Business School.

Did my feminist rage push her off track onto a wrong route? On the contrary, she has had a great career path, which I believe is partly because of this feminist spirit infused in her early, and of course her smart intellect. She has since worked in an international commercial bank, in the International Finance Corporation, a Breton Woods institution, and she has served as head of the She Trade Programme at the International Trade Centre, where she has worked with passion to ensure women in business have access to markets. Today, she is a chief of a division (Sustainable and Inclusive Value Chains) in the same institution, following a career path she dreamed of from the beginning. Like her mother and grandmother before her, she has broken the patriarchal gender stereotype of what a girl in Uganda is expected to become in a patriarchal world. She was able to do this because the framework of her upbringing set rules that would enable her to stand up and defy the system of patriarchy and its rules that are mostly barriers to girls' aspirations.

Patrice, her brother, did a master's of science in electrical and electronic engineering and a master's in digital communications systems. There was never a debate about that. Today, he is a self-employed private-sector man. He is proud to talk about how the majority of people in his company in management positions are women and how he constantly has to correct his clients when they insist on wanting to talk to "the manager," because they refuse to accept that the woman they have been referred to is the manager. He is not afraid to be in the kitchen, cooking for his family. This is possible because he grew up with a father who also broke barriers and made no distinction about women's or men's roles along the lines of the colonial patriarchal-based gender divide. This is how, together, we have chipped away at patriarchy. My feminism starts with me in my home, in my environment, together with those around me.

Not many girls and young women have had the benefit of growing up in feminist homes. An African woman is a bundle of relations that multiplies her roles as she grows up, sometimes to her breaking point, if she did not grow up in an empowering environment. She is told that "success" is getting a man (always only a man), getting married, and having the number of children *he* wants, then she'll be taken care of forever. This, irrespective of the instability of the marriages we see in Uganda today, plus domestic violence that grows more vicious every year. The woman is trained and reminded to be submissive and even to apologise for the violence her dissatisfied husband finds necessary to mete out, as a way of "disciplining" her. This is how patriarchy packages a "good successful woman." But as one of my mentees once remarked, "If you follow the popular definition of a 'successful' woman in Uganda, you are on your way to failure."

When I started working with girls directly, after my retirement, I began to understand and appreciate how girls are many times pushed to make choices that do not make sense. I once had a discussion with some girls in a local community in Nebbi, an area like all cultures in Uganda with very entrenched patriarchal mind-sets about the role of women. I was trying to understand from them why girls in the area marry when they are incredibly young.

The child marriage rate in the area was at 26.9 %. A girl of not more than fifteen years old, whose friend of the same age had dropped out of school, raised her hand to share the story of why her friend had left school to get married. She described how, in her home, her friend was the cook for her own family, the cleaner for her grandparents' compound, the nurse for her auntie, and the laundry girl and carer for her siblings.

One day, she told her friend, "I am leaving school to get married. I am doing all the things my mother is supposed to do in her home. I am doing all the things for my brothers that their wives are supposed to do. And I am serving everybody in my community, but without recognition. Why should I not have my own home?"

That is when I understood how the bundle of relations and the intersectionality of women's and girls' lives can have such impacts on them that they are forced to make choices that are sometimes beyond comprehension. It is because of that conversation that I decided part of the work we do at MEMPROW must include mind-set change of parents and communities, to start putting value on girls beyond the multiple roles they play.

I set up MEMPROW from a conviction that it is possible for every girl to have a good life. Even with my feminist consciousness about the power of patriarchy, I was unprepared for the impact it has on girls and young women. I also realised, by the time girls in Uganda become women, they have internalised and normalised the consequences of patriarchy to the point of paralysis, even when their lives depend on their fighting back. They have been brought up with no voice or agency to fight back, because defying patriarchy calls for punishment. My goal in mentoring young women is not just to awaken their consciousness to the power of patriarchy but also to stand up and defy its patriarchal negative norms and practices.

I have met girls studying in universities who explain away violence against them by their boyfriends as discipline from the boyfriend, because the Bible says she must submit. I have listened to schoolgirls explaining why they expect boyfriends of the same age, who are equally dependant on their parents, to buy them designer clothes. In one group discussion, one girl stood up and said, "If he cannot afford me, he cannot love me." The patriarchal mind-set, that a head of house means a male who has money is breeding a new form of patriarchy, one that makes love and marriage transactional in cash terms; with the man holding the power to provide.

I decided to take this conversation beyond schoolgirls to young women who are already in employment and being paid. The response was the same: "If you have a boyfriend, he has to give you money to prove he is capable of taking care of you when you get married."

What I learned in these conversations is that internalising and accepting patriarchal gender norms of masculinity and femininity has come to determine power relationships between partners in later life. This often leads to acquiescing to violence in these relationships. I believe this is why, in Uganda, violence against women and girls is still very high, with more than half of women (51%) aged 15-49 report having experienced physical violence; also, 22% of women, compared to 8% of men, have experienced sexual violence (Uganda 2016 Demographic Health Survey Uganda 2016).

What I learned, talking to girls and young women, convinced me that there is a need to support and train girls and young women how to unlearn the patriarchal mind-set that glorifies gender inequality. They have to grasp that accepting this normative framework means agreeing to a system that discriminates against and devalues women. We needed a sustained programme to train girls to value themselves and hold their heads up.

When we first meet the girls in our training, for example, they have exceptionally low aspirations, because the system has taught them they will be taken care of. For most of young women, the first goal is to get and keep a boyfriend who could become a husband to take care of her.

In discussions with the girls and young women in universities, one of the questions we usually ask is what their greatest fear at University is. They did not talk of academic failure or gender discrimination, or even fear of dropping out for lack of tuition fees. With very few exceptions, the greatest fear is "being chucked by a boyfriend" and the next greatest fear is becoming pregnant. We use this feedback to guide them into seeing that building relationships based on the expectation of being taken care of can come at a heavy cost. It impinges on your individual agency and voice; in an unequal power relationship, you cannot choose how somebody takes care of you.

We also integrated comprehensive sexual health and reproductive rights education into our curriculum, to give girls the means to choose when and how they become pregnant, without fear. It is incomprehensible that a university student is afraid of falling pregnant by accident in this era, with all the available family-planning facilities.

However, at MEMPROW with our feminist lens, we understand that is how the power of patriarchy works. It paralyses your decision-making processes and causes you to think you don't have a choice.

In Uganda, the education system is still discussing whether comprehensive sexual education should be taken into schools for adolescent girls and boys. This in spite of the fact that we have one of the highest teenage pregnancy rates in Africa, with one in every four girls experiencing teenage pregnancy (24%) at the national level and with some areas reaching 30.6%.[11] Policy guidelines are guided by patriarchal mind-sets. The argument is that the more knowledge girls have on sexuality and family planning, the more likely they are to become curious to practice and therefore become pregnant.

In all the schools where MEMPROW has established a mentoring programme and incorporated sexual health and reproductive rights training and information, reports show there has been a reduction in teenage pregnancy. The more information the girls received, the smarter the choices they made. I started an organisation for mentoring young women from a deep appreciation of knowing from experience that a good life is possible for women and girls. Working with young women on a full-time basis for the last eleven years, I have learnt that the more things change, the more they remain the same. Many of these girls have lost self-esteem and live with negative self-worth; they are

---

[11] "Our Children Our Future: National Forum on the State of the Ugandan Child Briefing Note." 2015.

taught to measure their worth within the patriarchal norm, where marriage is the prize, and the sooner you get it, the better.

In Uganda and many other parts of the world, marriage is seen as the golden solution by parents for their daughters. Getting her married to a "good" man who has financial prospects is seen as the ultimate goal. I have nothing against marriage; I myself was married to the same man, happily, for forty-six years. But when you go into this archetypical patriarchal institution without voice or agency and independent means, it will be a poisoned chalice.

To survive this system, first you must have the character to challenge the system and win. This is why, in my later years, I am investing my energy in working with young women and girls; to support them in developing character that enables them to stand up and make a choice. I am often asked when I plan to retire from all this and start enjoying myself. This is not work one can retire from; I watched my mother serving well into her eighties. My enjoyment and fulfilment come from knowing one girl is leading a life of her choice and is standing up against discrimination and oppression partly as a result of my work.

CHAPTER FOUR

LIP SERVICE IS NO SERVICE AT ALL

YOU CAN'T CHANGE THE WORLD of women and girls if you don't change the negative ways in which people think about them. Many men as well as women say the right things about equality but still have the mind-set that women and men cannot be equal. It is a form of resistance, when opponents of gender equality perceive it as a similarity between women and men. But even those who accept that women are equal in law and rights still believe women should be at home, raising children and submitting to men.

Raising children would not be a problem on its own, because women raise children even when they are not at-home moms. The problem is we still do not accredit value to the care work of women, even when we know the world survives on it.

In the West Nile region where MEMPROW does most of its work, we learnt that women are referred to as goal keepers. As a football fan, I was excited about this important title given to women in the community. It was not until I learned that the implication is that women sit at home, doing nothing and waiting for their husbands to bring "things" that I understood the salient and silent ways in which women's work is devalued. It is because of this that we decided to include gender-role analysis[12] into all our training in communities. With a gender role analysis, it is easy for women to situate their experience in a system of power and privilege. It also enables them to appreciate their self-worth, because the importance of the work they do suddenly gets visibility. We were also able to give a positive definition to goal keeping in line with the role of a goal keeper in football. Today, women understand that being a goal keeper implies they are bringing value in the family, because if you do not have a great goal keeper, there will be no success.

Uganda has the best laws on protecting girls and women's rights. The principle of gender equality is entrenched in the 1995 constitution, however, these laws are not transforming women's lives. This is because both the duty-bearers as well as rights-holders see women's and men's lives as well as their respective places through a patriarchal lens. Girls are still being married off at a young age to ensure women are being kept uneducated and having their life options limited. All this needs to change.

---

[12] Gender analysis refers to the variety of methods used to understand the relationships between men and women, their access and control to resources, their activities, and the constraints they face relative to each other. Gender analysis is an essential element of socio-economic analysis.

What I have learned is, if we want change so women may live in dignity without violence in their lives, we must dare to be different and challenge the patriarchal norms. Many of these are new norms of patriarchy that have been superimposed on our traditions by colonial mentalities concerning the place of a woman; they were supported by an exploitative colonial economy that took men from household production to a cash production, so they could pay taxes to the colonial government.[13] This was an economy that put money on a pedestal but devalued household production, which had been traditionally a joint activity of men and women in a household. This work became women's work, because men were taken out to work for money and to pay taxes. But women's work without pay subsidised men's work in the cash economy.

My research for my thesis, which focused on understanding gender relations and the household economies, showed this very clearly. In Uganda, women play a vital role in the country's rural agricultural sector, and they contribute a higher-than-average share of crop labour in the region. They also make up more than half of Uganda's agricultural workforce, and a higher proportion of women than men work in farming—76% versus 62%. Yet

---

[13] Article 12 of the Uganda agreement, 1900. In order to contribute to a reasonable extent towards the general cost of the maintenance of the Uganda Protectorate, there shall be established the following taxation for Imperial purposes; that is to say, the proceeds of the collection of these taxes shall be handed over intact to Her Majesty's representative in Uganda as the contribution of the Uganda province towards the general revenue of the Protectorate.

policy makers still pay lip-service to the importance of women in Uganda's agricultural development.

For example, the agricultural sector is among the lowest ranked sectors in the national budget. If women counted, perhaps budgetary allocations to agriculture and maternal health would be higher. This patriarchal economic structure still has detrimental results for women. It created a system of tax payment with a specific privilege of employment exclusively for men. Today, many still believe, if you are a man, you deserve to be employed first, because you will become the head of a family and must have access to money.

Until recently, and I am not sure that this has changed, the primary-school syllabus had a gendered question: "Who is the head of the family?" Woe to you, the student, if you gave a different answer to that of "father," even if you live in a single-female-headed household. In my gender training, I teach young women and men to question the concept of "head of household." When I ask, almost 100% of the learners say "father," including those without a father or a man in the home. This is in spite of the fact that households in Uganda are said to be at least thirty-percent female-headed; these statistics do not matter in policy and decision-making or allocation of national resources. The more things change, the more they remain the same.

The ugly side to the perception that all and only men must have access to money and must therefore be heads of households is that it created justification for discrimination against women in the labour sector. Until the late Sara Ntiro fought against the patriarchal norm by refusing less pay than her colleagues, in the late fifties, the colonial government salary structure assumed women needed less money. This changed when Dr. Ntiro, an Oxford graduate, challenged the system and told Mrs. Cohen, the wife of the then-Governor that she would rather go home than work for less than the men, when she had qualifications equal to theirs and was doing the same job as they were.

When formal institutions are managed with this patriarchal mind-set that can have negative consequences, especially for girls and women. For example, I work in a community in Uganda where girls' education is stopped too soon, mostly after Ordinary Level certificate. The explanation from the men and women, equally, is that educated women will have money and want to become heads of households, which is seen as a contradiction to the cultural norms. This mentality is denying generations of girls a good education and keeping the nation backward. In the same community, we train teachers about women's rights and gender bias so that they give equal opportunities to girls in their schools. In one training, I asked a group of eighty teachers whether they would marry a woman of equal education and the answer was the same for almost all the men in the room: they would not. The explanation given was that if she held equal qualifications, she would get the same salary; she would want to be the head of household and therefore would be difficult to discipline. Such is the power of patriarchy, that a family would reduce its standard of living in order to maintain male power.

The same mentality sustains unequal structures of privileges and discriminates against women in the workplace, when patriarchal mind-sets are brought into formal structures of work. When I worked at the Eastern and Southern African Management for Eastern and Southern Africa in Arusha, Tanzania, I carried out several researches [14] in corporate organisations in the region, (Uganda, Zambia, and Botswana) to establish the extent to which patriarchal mind-sets were used to define the roles and privileges of male and female staff. Women in management positions shared experiences of being requested to take notes or serve tea in meetings they were supposed to chair. Medical benefits were not given to married women in their employment, even when they were not working in the same organisation as their husbands. The explanation was the same everywhere: "Children belong to men; they should take care of them." It did not matter whether the women were single parents or not.

When I worked in Makerere University after I married, I battled with administration to get housing. I was expected to commute to the workplace for long hours, even though the University policy provided housing for all the professional staff. I was told that my husband was supposed to house me and not the other way round. I finally got the housing but came out feeling bruised from fighting for my right to housing. When I applied for a vacancy of an associate Professor, my head of department told me in no uncertain terms that I should not bother, because he was planning to recommend my male counterpart, irrespective of the fact that I had a Ph.D. and he did not. When I got the

---

[14] "Women and men of the African Corporate Organisation :African Management Development Forum," Volume 3, No. 1. March 1992.

promotion instead of his man, I became his enemy number one. I had broken the gender norms and challenged his patriarchal mind-set, while he had lost.

The power of patriarchy over women and lip-service to their rights are also exemplified by the persistence of the payment of bride wealth. My mother was married off at the age of sixteen in 1941, and the reason she agreed to be married off is because a man she hardly knew had already deposited cows in her father's compound. It was taboo for cows to be returned to the suitor. This is the story my mother told me when I was old enough to ask why she never completed her education at Gayaza High School, a great school that I, too, later attended and where I had one of the best of my life experiences.

Seventy-eight years later, in spite of the progress Uganda has made in securing girls' and women's rights through policies and laws, parents are still exchanging cows for their daughters and calling it a token of appreciation. Traditionally, a token was never more than two to three cows. Today, some parents calculate cows in terms of the number of years the daughter has stayed at school. In many places in Uganda, young girls are taken from school to marry because parents want cows; the value of a daughter is calculated in how many cows she can bring in. This is a mentality that still exists in the mind-set of most Ugandans.

A good example of this is when, in 2015, the issue of the payment of bride wealth was given attention through a legal challenge of the constitutionality of a customary practice of refunding the bride price, by MIFUMI, a human rights non-governmental organisation in Uganda. Uganda's

Supreme Court declared the practice of refunding bride wealth unconstitutional, in a six-to-one majority decision. However, it held the practice of paying a bride price as a condition for contracting a valid marriage in a four-to-one majority. The power of patriarchy is at work even in the mind-sets of the law makers and those who are supposed to give justice to women but who continue to pay lip service to women's rights. Under patriarchy, many norms and conditions of inequality remain consistent even as other changes occur, because we are all steeped in this system.

Women, no matter who they are, are victims of this system in one way or another. I too was bartered for cows in 1972, although unsuccessfully. When I took my boyfriend to introduce him to my parents before our wedding 3 weeks later, clansmen of my father saw an opportunity for getting cows. Culturally, the father is not the only beneficiary in the bride wealth game. My "uncles" sat with my husband to discuss how many cows he should pay while my parents looked with disinterest because they had not planned to barter me. My husband had just come back from Cambridge with no money to pay for the 10 cows they were asking for. My brother who had offered to go home with me to make the introductions official and well aware that I was not for sale stood up and told my uncles he was taking back his future brother-in-law if they did not stop the bartering. They were stunned and looked at my parents to intervene. Their silence showed that they approved my brother's intervention. They proved that their support to their daughter to be free was not lip service.

Tell your Story and Stand Tall

Women and men are born equal, but why is it that women are always told to stand and be counted? Why do we need this as an extra qualification?

The point is, as women we are marked,[15] so even when we stand, we are *not* counted. What I have also learned is that when you challenge and break gender norms, you have to win, otherwise the punishment can be heavy. This is one of the reasons most girls and women, even when they know they are getting a raw deal, prefer not to fight back.

I have also learnt that you must have certain qualities to challenge the patriarchal system. Personally, I have been successful in challenging patriarchal rules mostly because I have self-belief and positive self-worth. I was brought up in an empowering environment, where I was trained to understand that I deserve a good life with freedom of expression, high aspirations, and hard work. Education, and higher education for that matter, were necessary in order to stand up for a better life and service. Because of all

---

[15] "Women can't even fill out a form without telling stories about themselves. Most forms give four titles to choose from. 'Mr.' carries no meaning other than that the respondent is male. But a woman who checks 'Mrs.' or 'Miss' communicates not only whether she has been married, but also whether she has conservative values as well. Checking 'Ms.' declines to let on about marriage (checking 'Mr.' declines nothing, since nothing was asked), but it also marks her as either liberated or rebellious, depending on the observer's attitudes and assumptions." From *There is No Unmarked Women* by Deborah Tannen

this, I can sustain my feminist principles of independent thinking and challenge the system.

In general, women's life experiences are defined by violence or strategies to avoid violence. Women are survivors in spite of this. This is what I have learned working with women and girls; that in spite of the laws and the assurance that women are the mothers of the nation, we are almost on our own because we have minimal protection from gender violence.

A young woman turning up to report a case of sexual harassment or rape has to explain how and why it happened. If she turns up to a clinic to request for contraceptives and HIV/AIDS test, she is asked to bring the man she is sleeping with.[16] A wife reporting battering by the husband, either to law enforcement officers or clan heads, is required in some patriarchal cultures, to go back and do better, to please her husband so he stops beating her.

It is this learning that has helped us fine-tune the approach to our empowerment training at MEMPROW and introduce gender-role analysis to help the women learn to look at their lives from a wider perspective of patriarchal norms, mind-sets and practices. We developed an approach that combines building self-esteem and self-worth with enhancing cultural knowledge, as a way of understanding

---

[16] Once a young women turned up at health centre for a test for HIV/AIDS and was asked, "Why? Are you sleeping with men?" She had just completed MEMPROW's two-week social survival training, so she replied, "No, but it is my right to know my status." She stood up for her rights.

the power of patriarchy and bringing back dignity in women's lives, through exposing and analysing gender roles[17] in the community. The latter is also carried out in training with boys and men and has contributed greatly to transforming mind-sets.

William Easterly,[18] in his book *The Tyranny of Expert,* which he has labelled, "The intellectual journey toward a debate on autocracy versus freedom," has articulated that "Any approach to development will either respect the rights of the poor or it will violate them. One cannot avoid this moral choice by appealing to 'no ideological evidence-based policies' (a popular phrase in development today). Authoritarian development is also a pragmatic tragedy ... The technocratic illusion is that poverty results from a shortage of expertise, whereas poverty is really about a shortage of rights."

---

[17] A gender analysis includes information on women, men, girls, and boys in terms of their division of labour, roles and responsibilities, access to and control over resources, and their relative condition and position in society. It also involves looking at other norms for how gender may be expressed, including norms relating to sexuality and identity. A gender analysis should include social variables such as ethnicity, culture, age, and social class, and it should include both quantitative (statistics) and qualitative data (analytical and relative).

A gender analysis highlights specific vulnerabilities of women and men, girls and boys. It always has an empowerment perspective, highlighting the agency and potential for change in each group. Scope and methods vary. *SIDA Gender Analysis: principles and Elements,* 2015.

[18] William Easterly. *The Tyranny of Experts: Economics, Dictators, and the Forgotten Rights of the Poor.*

When we started working with communities in the process of transforming negative mind-sets, we were guided by the conviction that a society's cultural history and experiences matter; and that we were not starting from a blank slate. As a methodology of empowerment, we used storytelling, where stakeholders talked about what has changed and what is negatively impacting on the lives of girls and women. This proved to be transformative, because men and women, girls and boys were able to analyse good and bad practices in their community.

This was possible because we made it clear to our stakeholders that we were not experts on their culture or on what their aspirations were, and that they had a right to talk about what is not working and make suggestions on what could work for them. We also introduced training on human rights for them to understand that "individual rights were both an end in themselves and a means by which a free society solved many of their own problems" (Easterly).

Storytelling, another approach to training that we introduced has been the most impactful and transformative approach in our social-survival training of girls; and in our community empowerment programs in which we also work with women and men as well as boys. When women and girls, boys and men tell their stories, we use these to analyse the gender-relation issues and to uncover the power of patriarchy. Using their own experiences in their various intersectional contexts is a powerful process of understanding the source and cause of their lack of economic and social development, as well the different oppressions of girls and women.

One effective tool of sustaining discrimination and violence within patriarchal systems is silencing women's voices. Women are taught from childhood that they cannot voice their experiences of violence or exclusion from family decision-making matters in public, because it is a private matter. One tribe in Uganda has a saying, "Household matters are not aired out in public," and it is passed on by marriage counsellors to all the young women preparing for marriage. The separation of private and public life, while useful in many ways, is harmful when it defines domestic violence and gender-based discrimination as a private matter.

When we introduced storytelling in our training, it was like the proverbial "opening a can of worms": we broke the myth of the private and public. Girls and women were able to talk about the violences they were experiencing publicly. Without exception, every girl and woman, when asked to describe their defining moment, mentions their most common experience was about sexual and gender-based violence and discrimination. We introduced counselling in all our trainings as a strategy to manage the "can of worms" we were opening. Many of them—not only girls and women, but boys and men, as well—have lived with traumatic experiences and memories that they have never had an opportunity to talk about and place these experiences in the larger picture of patriarchy. Our commitment to safeguarding privacy for the girls and women we work with stops me from describing individual stories, but through telling stories, men and boys have come to appreciate that they, too, are victims of a system that gives them privilege.

Take an example of a man who has been taught to think that he is the sole provider. Most men have talked of losing self-esteem and having suicidal tendencies, but also using violence as a cover-up for their inadequacy. But they learned that this, too, is a patriarchal power privilege of men. This is because while a man can beat up his wife on the pretext that she has made him feel inadequate, a woman cannot beat her husband with an excuse that he makes her feel inadequate. Feeling emasculated is an excuse often given by men for beating their wives.

Through storytelling, both women and men come to understand how the power of patriarchy works negatively in their lives. They have been able to find solutions that are relevant to their contexts. The process is illustrated below.

STORYTELLING FOR HEALING, LEARNING AND BEHAVIOR CHANGE[19]

---

[19] Graphics by Immaculate Mukasa, the then-Programmes Director and Monitoring and Evolution expert, currently Executive Director of MEMPROW

Storytelling

An activity of writing, telling or reading an account of (past /present) events in someone's life.
Sharing and interpreting experiences.

Background

MEMPROW receives very many girls and women, victims of violence who have never had any opportunity to share their experiences, analyse their situations and related consequences to their own lives 'today and tomorrow,' impact on their children, dear ones, family, and community at large.

Why storytelling

Allowing and encouraging victims to engage in story telling constitutes a crucial part of transitional legal and political processes.
It is a method to reach values, cultural norms, and differences. MEMPROW also uses this methodology to interrogate negative sociocultural norms, heal victims and demand access to justice and protection of girls and women.

Important to note: Sometimes there are anti-stories. MEMPROW however maintains that the original storytellerowns her story and the unique experience therein.

Storytelling at MEMPROW: Generic process

- **Step 1**: •Girls, women, men and boys referred to MEMPROW
- **Step 2**: •Registration
  - •Introduction to MEMPROW Training and relevant topics
- **Step 3**: •Story Telling
- **Step 4**: •Interpreting and analysing experiences
- **Step 5**: •Lessons learnt by participants
- **Step 6**: •Commitments to behaviour change
- **Step 6**: •Evaluation of training / Learning days

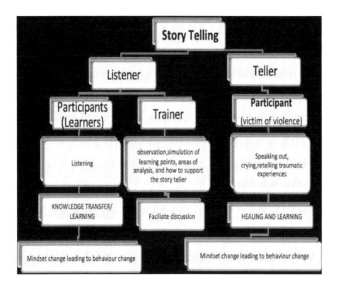

DISCUSSION	CONCLUSION
Embedded in each story are social-cultural norms and individual factors that influenced intonation by the story-teller, and participants' reaction. These factors included economic status, family background and education levels.	Storytelling is empowering for the story teller. S/he finds his/her voice. When it happens in safe spaces, story telling results in healing of story teller, and some of the listeners. It also results into family healing and reconciliation. With interpretation and analysis, story telling is a great method of learning. Story telling triggers action to promote safety of women and girls. The end result of the story telling can be behaviour change, and change of socio-cultural norms for protection of girls and women from violence.

CHAPTER FIVE

BALANCING ACT:

THERE IS NO SUCCESS WITHOUT SUCCESSION

Setting a Succession Goal and Creating a Plan to Achieve It

TRANSITION, AS WE ALL KNOW, is a necessary life process. Life and death are natural transitions. However, experience tells us that professional transitions are not easily accepted, even when we know it is time to make the change. We convince ourselves that we are not senile, that our minds are still sharp, and that we are more alert than the youth who, besides, do not have the experience we have.

When I tell people that I am finally retiring from active formal work, I am flattered that people tell me I do not look my age or old enough to retire. I am told I have the energy of the young. In a conversation with one of the office drivers, he asked me if MEMPROW would ever find someone with the same energy I have. I felt good about the fact that even staff appreciate my level of energy. My team members tell me I have the brain of an elephant, because I tend to remember details they have long forgotten. The joke between us is "Doctor, what do you eat?" But that is the catch: believing we cannot leave, unless we find somebody just like us to replace us.

When do we know it is time to make a transition? And how do we plan so that, as we exit, we leave succession plans that will ensure our successes?

I recently watched a television interview in which a senior citizen who is still involved in politics was trying to convince the interviewer that he was not yet too old for his position. He told of how he is still relevant and told a lot of jokes, but he was the only one laughing at them. Watching him, I kept thinking that it was time for him to retire from active politics; once you start explaining and justifying your relevance, perhaps you are no longer relevant. I often tell my children, if ever they catch me sleeping during a meeting, they should use their rights to remove me from public office.

I have no problem making professional transitions. My rule is that I should not spend more than ten years doing the same thing. I also made a commitment to myself that I would not work in an institution where I have to fight to be allowed to do what I was employed to do in the first place. In my professional history, I left an interesting institution, ACBF, after two years, when I felt I could no longer bring to the table what I was recruited to bring, which was working to ensure that gender justice and equality objectives were integrated into the organisation's work.

In this chapter, I want to share MEMPROW's journey towards successful change management and its transition from a founder-led organization to an organisation led by young women who were groomed and mentored within the organisation. It tells a journey of how learning, feminist leadership, and partnerships were brought together, turning what could have been a challenging transition experience into a pleasant one.

Planning for change and transition: what does it take? In life, some transitions are easier than others. Birth and death are the easiest, because one does not have a choice. Professional transitions are more difficult, as they involve decisions that could make or break your profession and, let's face it, your livelihood. In my personal experience, deciding to exit MEMPROW, the last centre stage of my professional active life, has been the most difficult.

I began an emotional transition and change-management thought process in 2016, a landmark year in my life, when I suddenly lost my husband. It was a year of both great loss and awakening. I started questioning myself: what if that had been me? Would the organisation have been left in a crisis? He and I had started MEMPROW together and had provided the leadership needed, although his had gradually changed into an advisory role. When death came as close as it did, to someone who was so near and not much older than I, it occurred to me I needed to prepare my team at MEMPROW for my professional transition. I had to purposely plan for my succession and move MEMPROW from a founder-led organisation to a new leadership. If not, the success of MEMPROW over the years would be obliterated in the crisis of unexpected change.

In 2017, I decided to go beyond thinking about transition and went into action to start the change process. My confidence to embark on this journey lay in the fact that we had created a MEMPROW team of young women who functioned perfectly. As a coordination Secretariat, there was no doubt in my mind they could continue to function. However, my decision to plan for transition was a fulfilment of some of my feminist core values. The first is that I must invest in capacity building and trust the women I have worked with and mentored to carry on with MEMPROW's agenda. I was certain that they would, in turn, empower and give other girls and young women a voice to challenge and transform a patriarchal society that sustains discrimination, oppression, and gender inequality. Stewardship is another core value in feminism to which I am committed. Stewardship has many meanings, but in organisations, it could refer to the "responsibility of managing the staff and resources, and caring for or improving them with time." Hanging on to leadership and then suddenly leaving an organisation in a crisis is a mark of poor stewardship.

Planning for transition and change, from leading MEMPROW to total retirement, has not been easy. I still carry the same passion and energy for mentoring girls and young women and for fighting to eliminate gender violence and discrimination. In this section, I would like to take the reader through the three-year journey of learning and process for the change and transition we went through, both at an individual and organisational level.

We were fortunate to have and work with partners such as the African Women Development Fund (AWDF), Medical Mondiale (MM), American Jewish World Service (AJWS), and Open Society Initiative for Eastern Africa (OSIEA), and United Artists for Africa (USA), who all invested in our transition and change-management processes with both capacity-building and financial support. Indeed, the whole process of change management was guided by lessons from training given to me as Executive Director of MEMPROW by Medica Mondiale. It is through my participation in the annual Feminist Leadership Training, organised by MM for its partners, that I began to recognise mistakes I was making, and the lack of preparedness with which I was approaching my exit from MEMPROW. I realised that a well-intended agenda was heading for disastrous results and then set about approaching change and transition professionally.

In 2017, MEMPROW staff and board members formally embarked on the process of replacing the Founder/Executive Director. The first step in successful change and transition, I learned, was to identify a sponsor, someone who recognised it was necessary and would leave no stone unturned to make sure it happened. When the sponsor is the person seeking to exit, the change process is much more pleasant and easier to accept by the person moving out. In MEMPROW's case, because I, the founder and leader, was the sponsor of the change, the process *had* to be successful. I also found that change is easier if the founder has no "founder's syndrome" and has a personal transition plan, as well. For example, I did not depend on MEMPROW for my livelihood. Once I was convinced that I needed to exit, I set about preparing myself and the team for acceptance of change. Many people have asked me if I really will retire and leave the organisation. My response is that I must and will: the survival of the organisation depends on my exit.

Why Transition Change in Leadership?

"There is no Success without Succession."

I led MEMPROW as Founder-Executive Director from its beginning, in 2008, until 1 April 2020. Over the years, as founding Executive Director, I was deliberate in building an organisation that gained credibility in empowering and mentoring young women for agency, leadership, and participation. My international identity and high professional profile, as a Founder, were major positives for resource mobilisation. The advantages of this identity are that, as ED, I had enough experience and knowledge, as well as a vision that enabled me to invest in hiring and mentoring young women without fear of competition.

This is a practice that, although it had great value in creating leadership, had its weakness in that the founding ED remained the face of the organisation for a long time. But change in succession was necessary, irrespective of the challenges the organisation could face.

One of the difficulties in succession is that grooming emerging leaders can take longer than expected.

Fundamentally, as a founding ED, I began to recognise that younger leaders would not feel ready to take full leadership if they continued to operate under a shadow of the founding ED. The overall challenge, then, was to convince the team that they were ready and it was time for the Founder/ED to step out and hand over leadership to the younger generation. I assured the MEMPROW team they did not need to walk in my shoes; what they needed was to use their own shoes and make their own footprints.

Another reason for change was related to my personal desire to counter negative perceptions of Founders held among the younger generations I was mentoring. In Uganda, founding members, both men and women, are perceived as leaders who do not leave positions of leadership in the organisations they have started. There are many examples where this is true. I recognised this could be a hindrance to the change process, and to effective handing over leadership in the organisation. As a feminist, I was determined not to validate the negative perception, and instead chose to be the key stakeholder in championing and implementing the change. Further, MEMPROW is an organization for mentoring young women. I, as the founding ED was already a very senior citizen, which, although not an immediate challenge in itself, could pose a challenge with the generation gap, especially in perceptions of what the girls and young women needed in order to be groomed for leadership. For example, one essential area of expertise is media skills; here, the younger generation has an advantage over the older generations. Indeed, the art with which my team has employed digital communications in sustaining the work during the pandemic has shown that I was right to hand over during this crisis.

The major push for accelerated leadership change, however, came because of the awakening due to my personal tragedy, when I lost my husband, who had been a great supporter and co-founder of MEMPROW. We had been together for forty-six years, and both of us had enjoyed good health. One Monday morning, I took him to hospital, and by Tuesday morning, he was gone.

I came away from this experience with one major question. What if it had been me? My answer was I would have left the organization in an anticipated crisis. I needed to start thinking for a planned exit, because, without planned succession, MEMPROW's gains could be lost overnight.

What did we do? And how?

Once it became clear that leadership change was a necessary, positive step, we embarked on this process and decided to treat it as a project with a beginning and an end; in addition, we identified key activities and stakeholders for a successful change. This process focused on several areas. We defined the key activities as:

✴ Building a resourced Executive Director's Office:

When Mr. Tadria and I started MEMPROW, we wanted it to be a place for us to give to others. We donated office space for the initial three years and decided not to take a salary or any benefits.

As we started thinking of transition and change, we had to face the fact that heading MEMPROW could no longer be a voluntary, though full-time job. Resource mobilisation became a critical activity in the processes of change. We also needed resources to undertake change-focused activities that will be described later.

We set about building a fully resourced ED's office with a salary. This became a focus for resource mobilisation. Our partners—AWDF, OSIEA, AJWS and Medica Mondiale—quickly bought into the idea and our process for change, and they have enabled us to manage the process effectively and positively. Because the team of partners held similar feminist values and vision for leadership, the goal of resource mobilisation was easily achieved.

Providing continuous learning and mentoring:

The process of institutionalising change included continuous mentoring and learning that involved both staff and Board members in several activities including:

* **Our learning:**

Our learning involved dialogues with leaders and staff of organisations that had made successful transitions from founding-ED-led organisations, notably Akili Dada in Kenya, as well as TASO, Akina Mama w'Africa (AMWA), Social Transformation Institute (STI), and International Peace Centre; all of them based in Uganda. From the Learning Visits, strengthening of policies stood out as a key area to be given attention in the process of transition.

We immediately put this learning in practice by identifying policy gaps and then worked to put all the necessary policies in place to address possible pitfalls that were identified as major constraints to positive and effective transition change management. Another lesson we learned is that the abrupt departure of an incumbent ED can disrupt the process of transition and render it negative. So, we instituted a process of mentoring for both staff and board.

The Founding Executive Director also participated in an International Learning Space provided by Medica Mondiale, MEMPROW's partner in fighting stigma and providing trauma healing for child-mothers. Designed for partners leading and managing women's organisations, the training programme provided important knowledge about feminist leadership and different styles of leadership, as well as basic principles of change management. From these training sessions, I came to be conscious of the fact that transition from a Founder Member comes with mind-set challenges, including fears of failure.

I shared my learning with staff and agreed to approach the process of transition management as a people process, as well as a structural change process. We learned that change is about what employees experience personally within themselves. Therefore, we introduced structured learning, focusing on getting staff to do self-reflection on what could block successful institutionalisation of change. The result of this is that both the staff and Founder/ED have gone through training that has seen them make significant shifts in their mind-set, moving from the "unfreeze" stage, per the graphic below.

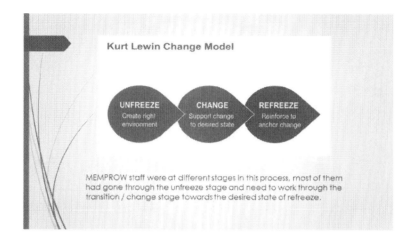

During this initial stage of change management, we also undertook a skills capacity and financial systems assessment. We established that, as a secretariat, the existing MEMPROW team had the skills necessary to manage the organization. The financial systems assessment indicated a need for strengthening, and that was taken as an urgent action. MEMPROW systems have been overhauled according to the gaps identified.

Board members participated in structured learning sessions aimed at strengthening our governance and common understanding of MEMPROW's human rights-feminist approach. Hope Chigudu, an internationally recognized Organizational Development Specialist and Leadership Coach, provided direction in the learning process. She was selected for this task because she worked as a coach for MEMPROW over a long period of MEMPROW's existence. She is also known as a woman of integrity with a knack for putting bad news on the table without causing shock. She was able to take both the board and the staff to a common understanding of why we do what we do and why board members can only serve on the board if their ideology of human rights and feminist leadership are in tandem.

* **The mentoring process:**

This stage was an automatic transition from the learning stage, as we started working towards mentoring staff to support the change to its desired state: acceptance and ultimate institutionalization. Mentoring took place in two phases, before and after recruitment.

In the first phase, time was allocated to staff to discuss their fears and share their future dreams about their organisation and to build scenarios of possibilities and impacts. In one innovative retreat session, the team came up with a powerful visual art presentation of their vision of MEMPROW, when change had been institutionalised (see picture below). It represents a vision of a successful MEMPROW, fishing out more girls in an unending river journey, with a bright future represented by the sun and owning an own building standing out in purple feminist colours.

Regular meetings between the board and staff were also organized, and these provided regular check-ups on levels of acceptance. When we had registered a reasonable level of acceptance (see diagram below), we agreed it was time to take the process forward and advertised for the job of Executive Director.

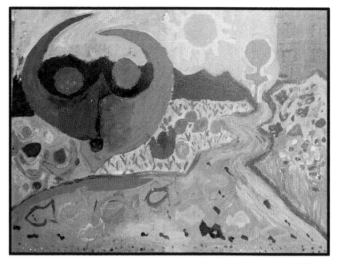

Painting of the staff vision of the future, painted by the staff[20]

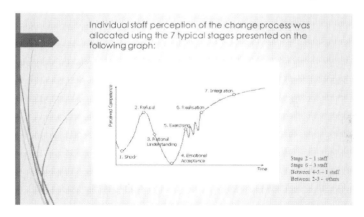

---

[20] In their explanation, the painting depicts a brighter future seen in the rising sun. The purple building and expanding river indicate organisational expansion with feminism at the core, hence the purple colour. The multitude of fish in the river stand for the many more girls they would continue to fish for.

127

✳ Staff road map for transition:

The board took leadership for recruitment, but the MEMPROW staff provided what they desired as the map for leadership Transitional and Change Process Milestones:

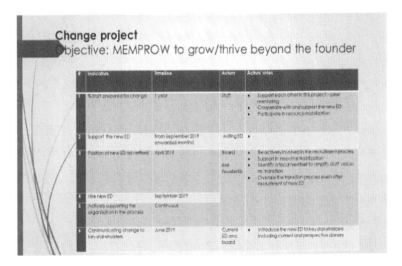

✳ Successful recruitment and leadership change:

In January 2020, three years after embarking on the process of change, the board was finally able to select and hire a new ED who assumed her office on 1 April 2020. The internal candidate stood out as the best, which affirmed the value of internal capacity-building and mentoring.

The conclusion of recruitment ushered in a second stage of mentoring. This focused on one-on-one staff mentoring through telephone calls and face-to-face meetings. It included a joint staff and board retreat for bonding and team building, where board members discussed their roles in ensuring effective institutionalisation of the change. They made commitments to support resource mobilization and described skills they would bring in. Staff meetings were organized to identify gaps and skills needed and to fill those left by staff taking new positions.

What was the first mentoring session like? Together with staff, we focused on imagining the future and discussing MEMPROW's preparedness against the current trends and leadership challenges. We started with an analysis of what the team was bringing to the table that would cement the organisation, recognizing that internal shifts create gaps.

The following represents consensus of how the team looks like in totality:

Passionate, care for each other, receptive, welcoming, knowledgeable, good at following up, reliable, generous, nurturing, commitment to work, pay attention to details, dynamic, get work done, truthful, beat deadlines, great networking skills, grounded in theory on issues they work on, fully aware of their responsibilities

It was agreed that, based on the above, the team I was leaving at MEMPROW was well positioned to steer the organisation to the next level of growth.

In our discussion, we acknowledged there would be a gap created by staff moving into leadership, therefore those taking their positions would need to be oriented and supported to do the work. The biggest concern, however, was that some sporadic donors might end relationships when the Founder/ED finally retired. It was agreed that effective communication would be important in mitigating negative perceptions and fear among stakeholders. MEMPROW, we all agreed, had a strong base of partners with shared feminist values, and this would keep the team working and focused on the vision of the organisation.

The transition and change process was not without challenges. First, the pool of applicants with the necessary experience and quality was extremely limited. But the biggest challenge came after selection of a candidate who looked like the best-skilled person to lead the organisation. Within a week of further due-diligence checks, there were clear indications that the best candidate did not meet MEMPROW's ethical standards. It was agreed that MEMPROW would suffer from collateral reputational damage if we went ahead with hiring the initial candidate. The board had to go back to the drawing board and call for new applications.

MEMPROW prides itself in the fact that it has zero tolerance to corruption, fraud, and theft. As a feminist organisation, we have worked hard to make sure we are an "organisation with a soul," where staff and every person we come into contact with is treated with respect and dignity. These are the principles that guided our board members' decision to reopen the recruitment. My team and I were, of course disappointed, especially me, who had finally been looking forward to a well-deserved rest after more than fifty years of service. I was requested to hold fort until a new, and more appropriate person was recruited. The board asked for new applications and finally selected a winning candidate.

My exit from MEMPROW took place on 31 March 2020 and came as an anti-climax. It was the first day of the total shut-down in Uganda because of the COVID-19 pandemic. As a team, we had planned to have an exit with a bang, in my home, where I would teach everybody how to make a Christmas cake. For a couple of years, I had been sharing my homemade Christmas cake with the team, and I had promised I would leave them the legacy of making and sharing the Christmas cake. This was not to be. Instead, my exit was marked by what could be described as a handover letter to the team; online. The new norm of communication of 2020.

From: Dr. Hilda Mary Tadria, Founder and outgoing ED

To: Ms. Immaculate Mukasa, Incoming ED;
Sarah Nakame, Programmes Director
And the entire MEMPROW staff

March 31, 2020 is a landmark day. It is the day I end my engagement with MEMPROW as the Founding ED since 2008. On 1 April, Immaculate Mukasa will take over as the new Executive Director.

I will no longer be your reference point. I exit this position to join the board of the organisation with mixed feelings. The feelings are of both joy as well as sadness. Sadness because of loss of a space that I love and value so much. It is a space that has brought meaning to my service; I have enjoyed the work as well as working with a great team. It is also a feeling of joy because I know, together, we have made a difference, and that by exiting, my success is made possible by succession from you. I am confident that what I am leaving behind is a shared vision that will survive.

First, I want to thank you, Immaculate, especially for putting yourself out for leadership. From the day I met you, I knew I was meeting a woman of value. You have brought professionalism in programme planning, implementation, as well as monitoring and evaluation. These are rare skills you brought to the table. You are going into leadership, a place where you will need to focus on doing the right thing and guiding the team to do things right. I hope it will bring as much joy to you as it brought me these last twelve years.

Secondly, the MEMPROW family, Nelly, Sarah, Fred, Lillian, Michael, Richard, Doris, Stella, Patience, Robert, Mercy, we did this together. You are an amazing team of positive women and men: flexible, supportive, joyful, and caring; a true feminist team. I do not know a workplace that has so much laughter in its corridors and offices as MEMPROW has. I have watched you all grow to be comfortable in your shoes. You do not need mine: wear yours, and they will take you on a longer journey.

You know and love what you do; so I am ready to let go. I am confident as I step out that MEMPROW will survive and thrive, because I know you are not doing this for me. You are doing this for your daughters, sisters, mothers, aunties, grandmothers. And you are doing this for yourself, because it makes a difference in the lives of girls/women and hopefully brings meaning to your life.

What have I learned from this process?

Never take anything for granted, plan for transition and change, engage your team, and most of all approach the prospect of change positively. This was made very clear to me when, in one of the mentoring sessions, the team came up in a painting with a visual vision of how their organisation would look like after the change. It portrays optimism and hope, growth and more opportunities. I knew then that there was nothing to fear, except fear itself.

CHAPTER SIX

MAKING A DIFFERENCE

I WAS ONCE TOLD by a wise friend that I was not put on Earth to fix the world. This is when I told this person that my retirement plan was to start an organisation to mentor girls so that they can safeguard their rights. Interestingly, in a recent conversation with my doctor about my plans to retire in the near future, he gave me another interesting perspective.

"Why are you retiring?" he asked.

"I need to rest," I replied.

He then set about telling me why retiring was an awfully bad idea. "The reason human beings go to bed is so they can get up and go to work. What will your purpose be for going to bed when you retire?"

I could not stop laughing, but I got the point. I needed to plan my retirement, as my team at MEMPROW urged me to do. I may not be the same actively engaged person in future again, I may not have changed the world, but I believe I have contributed in many different ways.

How and where have I made a difference?

I started MEMPROW hoping to make a difference in the lives of girls and contribute to reducing feminist ideological gaps between young and older feminists; some of our achievements have gone beyond my expectations. We have contributed to policy development, transformed negative cultural norms, and enhanced protection for vulnerable girls, while building a strong feminist movement of young women who are already taking up leadership in spaces they occupy.

In working with girls and young women, we based our approach on a strong conviction that mentoring and empowerment[21] of young women at a young age would build their capacity to stand up against patriarchal discrimination and oppression. This is consistent with my belief that the "comprehension of oppression is 'indispensable' to a new vision of the world based on justice and freedom."

The training programme for girls and young women focused on attitude change, especially their negative attitudes about themselves and low self-worth they had assimilated from a patriarchal environment. We also focused on building their knowledge of their rights, and we strengthened their entrepreneurship skills so they can be

---

[21] I use empowerment in this context to mean the following: "Empowerment" is defined as "the process of becoming stronger and more confident, especially in controlling one's life and claiming one's rights."

economically independent. The package was branded as a "Social Survival Training Programme."

Although the organisation's mission talks about girls and young women, in executing our work, we were guided by our learning and understanding that girls and women experience sexism/patriarchy and its repercussions differently depending on their social position in society, ethnicity, nationality, sexual orientation, age, ability, religion, and other attributes. We combined the mentoring and empowerment programmes for girls and young women with a community training programme on gender and human rights that sought to influence prevailing negative patriarchal norms and values within Uganda's socio-cultural environments. Learning from experience, we recognised that other levels of society must be affected for lasting efficacy. The imperative was to build supportive gender-aware and responsive institutional structures, facilities, and social environments in which adolescent girls and young women are supported to attain their aspirations.

MEMPROW was not set up as a service provider, and it cannot be expected to meet all the needs of young women. Our existence and niche hinges on preventing violence against young women and dismantling negative patriarchal mind-sets and norms which are systemic barriers. Weare very much aware that its (violence) causes are many and interrelated. Violence is directed at an individual based on her biological sex, gender identity, or her refusal to adhere to perceived or patriarchal socially defined norms of femininity. It includes physical, sexual, and psychological abuse; threats; coercion; arbitrary deprivation of liberty;

and economic deprivation, whether occurring in public or private life.

Violence against women and girls takes on many forms and can occur at any time. For many girls and women, it can be throughout one's lifecycle, from the prenatal phase through childhood and adolescence, the reproductive years, and old age. Patriarchy sits right at the centre of violence against women. This is why, in our work, MEMPROW looks at patriarchy along with class, ethnicity, age, location, sexuality, and other factors to shape an intersectional approach to violence and, conversely, empowerment or "liberation" of young women.

The organisation builds girls' and young women's leadership capabilities so they can stand out, mobilise, and amplify their political influence and demand for equitable distribution of resources, freedom from violence, and responsive and accountable institutions. MEMPROW's concept of what empowerment is simple, but the organisation provides the tools and space for people to understand the politics of their problems, and for them to act, individually or collectively, towards sustained solutions that improve their lives. The tools include political awareness, positive self-esteem, and relevant skills such as the confidence to use their voice and make smart choices.

MEMPROW's work has been based on the awareness that empowerment cannot be handed to anyone, but awareness can be raised.[22] It is possible for girls to learn

---

[22] MEMPROW Story: A young sister to the Women's Movement is born! She is called MEMPROW: Hope Chiggudu was commissioned to

what requires their own engagement in the process and to realise and accept that there is something to be achieved and somewhere positive to reach. This is only possible through greater understanding and comprehension of how oppression works and where it thrives. The methods we used for this empowerment included dialogues, storytelling, and training to develop life skills. We committed to working with one girl at a time, providing sustained mentoring, because we knew that one size does not fit all.

It is important to note that people get empowered differently and at different paces depending on issues of class, gender, sexual orientation, and ethnicity. It is also true that measuring empowerment is not a simple task. Traditional quantitative indicators of success often give an inadequate reading. MEMPROW is still refining its metrics to gauge the extent to which they have accomplished elements of the empowerment they seek through their work. However, to date, we can proudly say we have reached 20,000 girls directly. All of them have reached somebody; their testimonials produced in this book[23] are proof that they have self-agency,[24] a voice, and they are

---

document the achievements of MEMPROW at the 10th Anniversary. Some of the success stories are picked from this documentation.

[23] The testimonials have been reproduced with support from MEMPROW staff members and permission from the girls and young women who shared their stories of change.

[24] Self-agency, also known as "personal agency" in psychology, is a term that describes the feeling of being in control of our actions and the consequences this has on our lives. It is the power and ability to filter out

actively involved as leaders and transformers of negative social norms. I count this as one of my major contributions: building a community in which girls and young women have positive self-worth, can speak out, challenge oppression and inequality; and enjoy their rights with increased aspirations.

I got to learn and appreciate the importance of self-agency during my research for my Ph.D. Thesis[25] in 1985. When one is privileged with education and a well-paying institutional job, one is likely to believe they have a monopoly of self-agency. I was disabused of this idea by a woman who had never been to school and whose tool of work was a hoe and a garden for her work place. In a focus group discussion with a group of such women, I expressed sympathy when they talked about their abusive husbands.

One of the women laughed loudly, mocking my displaced sympathy. She then looked at me and said, "Nyabo (meaning madam), when my husband shows aggression, I pick up my hoe and disappear the whole day, leaving him to fend for himself. I know he cannot cook, but he also knows he cannot ask me where I am going, once I

_____

unwanted noise, find emotional and physical balance, think more clearly, and advocate for yourself. Self-agency is power, seeing as success in life is virtually impossible without it. Being an agent of your life means knowing where you are and what's happening to you, as well as having the ability to model circumstances. www.toomanly.com/what-is-self-agency-psychology-and-why-is-it-important/.

[25] "Changing Economic and Gender Issues among the Peasants of Ndejje and Sseguku in Uganda" by Hilda Mary Kabushenga Tadria, May 1985.

pick up my hoe. By the time I come back at the end of the day, he will have cooled down and let me live my life. On the other hand, I feel sorry for you educated women. When your husband gets angry and abusive, he gets up and gets into his car and leaves you seething with anger. When he decides to come back, you are the one who will apologise. So who do you think you should feel sorry for?"

It is also this group of women who told me to stop coming dressed as a privileged civil service woman, because I would raise suspicions that I had come either to spy for the government or spoil the women in the village. This perception would lose me access for my research.

Rotarian Samuel Frobisher Owori (RIP),[26] in his Rotary International president-nominee's acceptance remarks to the 2017 Rotary International Convention, said, "But truth must be told. In the process of doing well, we are the biggest beneficiaries, because our lives change. We become better people and enjoy that intrinsic satisfaction to which we cannot put a price. It is true that 'One profits most who serves best.'"

---

[26] RI PRESIDENT-NOMINEE'S ACCEPTANCE REMARKS Sam F. Owori, 14 June 2017. Owori, a member of Rotary Club of Kampala, was only the first Ugandan and second African to be elected President of Rotary International, a humanitarian service organisation that unites leaders committed to improving lives and bringing positive, lasting change to communities around the world. Unfortunately, he passed away a month later, on July 13, 2017

Indeed, if truth be told, I have been a beneficiary in large measure. Today, I have three adopted daughters[27] I met through my work with MEMPROW and who call my home their home. Today I am richer because of what they have brought to my life, and I cannot put a price on it.

I met each of them at different times in different institutions. One was a fourteen-year-old girl in a public school in Kampala; she was vibrant and dreamed of being a musician. Another one, about seventeen years old, was in a religious-based high school; she was highly intelligent, challenging, and angry with herself and everybody. The third one was older, at university, and had a pride about her that was infectious.

They all became victims of sexual violence in their homes, where they should have been protected, and found themselves seeking refuge at my doorstep. The fourteen-year-old had been raped in her father's home by a stranger to her who she believes was brought in by her stepmother. By the time she came to me, she was five months pregnant and so it fell to me to find a home where she would be nurtured to delivery. The seventeen-year-old had been on her long vacation, waiting to join university, but was experiencing extreme trauma after sexual violence and could no longer live in the environment where trauma was constant. All three had no one to turn to but MEMPROW.

Sometimes, fate prepares you for the unknown. All three girls had fascinated me in our earlier encounters, and

---

[27] I have their permission to talk about how and why I adopted them.

I often thought of them, wondering how their lives had panned out, after we left. When they came to MEMPROW, each at a different time, and insisted they wanted to talk to me and not the counsellor, I was excited until I saw their faces. I sat in my chair stunned, wondering what had hit them. The light that shone from their faces when I first met them had been snuffed out. I listened to their stories, each at different times but with a similar story of sexual violence; I knew I could not send them back to where they came from. This is when feminist consciousness had to be translated into feminist action and support.

I invited them home, looked for financial support for them to finish their education. Today, two of them are graduates, one with a master's degree and one an independent entrepreneur. The once-teenage mother who we supported with counselling and help for a safe delivery has a diploma and is self-employed. They are all standing tall, and they are my daughters. Together they form a formidable support team for each other, even though they are different ages and from different backgrounds. They are family, sisters, and daughters in my home. Indeed, "One Profits Most Who Serves Best."

How I Made a Difference, Seen Through Others' Eyes

I have made a difference in the lives of many girls and women as well as those of boys and men, at different times and in different places. Through my professional life and the work of my organisations, I know I contributed to transforming negative community mind-sets to gender equality, which has led to new policies for protecting girls and women's rights. My championing of deliberate planned change and successful transfer of leadership within my organisation, MEMPROW, has proved that Founder members are capable of investing in the grooming leaders to succeed them and that they can move on and hand power over to a new crop of leaders successfully.

In the next section of this chapter, I present a snapshot of the contributions and changes I and my team at MEMPROW have made through our work, seen through the eyes of other people who have been on this journey with me.

MEMPROW seen through Professor Sylvia Tamale's[28] eyes

Alesi stood out among the participants in the feminist workshop I facilitated in 2019 in Kampala. Her critical intelligence, self-confidence, and tough no-nonsense attitude was palpable. So much so that, afterwards, I approached her in a bid to know her better. It all made sense when I later learnt that she was a "MEMPROW Girl," as the young women who have been mentored by the organization MEMPROW fondly identify themselves. Alesi is emblematic of the mark MEMPROW has made on the crop of Uganda's young women who have been fortunate

---

[28] Professor Sylvia R. Tamale is a fearless human rights defender and feminist; she is also one of the first technical resource persons at MEMPROW, going back to 2018. She is a Ugandan academic and was the first female dean in the Law Faculty at Makerere University, Uganda.

enough to go through its hands. She is a typical example of the fruits that have blossomed from MEMPROW's work in the last twelve years.

MEMPROW Girls have rocked boats in the patriarchal waters that wash over Uganda's communities. Many may not know it, but the chain reaction effect of the 2018 sexual harassment "movement" that exploded on various university campuses in Uganda was ignited by MEMPROW Girls. It led to a nationwide survey of sexual harassment in Ugandan schools by Parliament, tighter policies against sexual harassment, and the dismissal of many sexual predators from various educational institutions.

Sexual violence was part of the discussion I facilitated in a MEMPROW young feminist convening in 2015. A group of students from Makerere University's School of Statistics and Planning approached me over the lunch break and related horrendous stories of sexual abuse at the hands of one notorious lecturer whose predatory behaviour was legendary at the school. His colleagues knew about his exploitative ways, as did the woman who sold chewing gum and pens on the veranda outside the school. First-year female students were warned about this lecturer during the freshers' orientation by fellow students: "Steer clear of Mr. Brian Musaga throughout your stay here!" Stories of Musaga's predatory behaviour poured forth for years. Despite such notoriety, Musaga continued harassing with impunity. Well…, until he encountered a MEMPROW Girl.

Justine recorded Musaga's propositions and demands for sexual favours. Unlike many victims before her, she was willing to come forward, and she dropped the "bombshell" against Musaga. MEMPROW had given her the courage and the voice to stand up against a powerful predator who acted as if he was above the law.

I helped Justine to lodge a formal complaint against Musaga. The Vice-Chancellor instituted an ad hoc committee to investigate Musaga. Five more victims mustered the courage to tell their stories to the committee, and eventually Musaga was dismissed from the university. The media publicity given to this case had a domino effect within and outside Makerere University. More sexual predators were suspended from Makerere. The head teacher of Kibuli Senior Secondary School was also dismissed, after investigations revealed he had abused his students for decades. For Makerere University, the process culminated in a comprehensive investigation of the issue and a total overhaul of its policy against sexual harassment in 2018.

These are a few examples to show how MEMPROW has achieved its goal of amplifying the voices of young Ugandan women, building their agency and influence. Obviously, there is still plenty of work to be done in wading through the patriarchal waters, but the ripples initiated by MEMPROW continue to radiate slowly but surely. A decade's work by one organization will not cause seismic shifts in the structural patriarchal-capitalist landscape that have shaped our society over millennia. However, with organizations like MEMPROW dotting the continent, Africa will doubtless begin to register real changes.

By shifting the mind-sets of young women, MEMPROW, through careful processes of unlearning and relearning, is taking the first crucial steps towards decolonising our societies. From enhancing awareness about sexualities to laying bare social survival skills, there is no taboo subject for MEMPROW Girls.

Historically, the feminist movement has tended to attract women from the humanities and social sciences and not from the physical sciences. The detrimental colonial policy that arranges knowledge in silo disciplines is partly responsible for this. The fact that MEMPROW works across disciplines has transcended the stereotypes, stepping forth as transformative and transdisciplinary in its approach. The new crop of emerging feminists in Uganda are likely to be less constrained by disciplinary boundaries, inter-professional politics, or even generational dynamics, thanks to MEMPROW and a few other organizations that have taken conscious steps to overcome these challenges.

Through its intergenerational mentoring programme, MEMPROW has fostered healthy feminist relationships across the age spectrum. The participants of their Young Feminist Convenings are inclusive of all gender and sexual orientations, as well as sex workers, underprivileged students from upcountry, and other social minorities. Young activists mingle with students and fresh-faced idealists; social barriers are broken. All this allows MEMPROW Girls to have a comprehensive and complex understanding of feminist issues and to theorize the linkages between gender, sexuality, and oppression.

Needless to say, most of the work MEMPROW does invokes intense emotional and psychological reaction from the participants. In the beginning, the organization did not appreciate the intensity and depth of emotional stress that they had to deal with, particularly young women who had directly and/or indirectly experienced gender-based violence. Once MEMPROW realized the pandemic proportion of violence against girls, including their own trainees, they embarked on engaging with psychologists to provide counselling services.

The next challenge they faced was finding feminist psychologists who would appreciate the issues and provide effective support. There were none in Uganda! So MEMPROW identified a few psychologists and counsellors and offered to train them in feminist theory and practice. I facilitated some of these remarkably interesting sessions with psychologists. This is another example to show how flexible MEMPROW can be and its ability to rise to any challenge in practical ways.

In short, my experience with MEMPROW for the past twelve years has been one of wonderment, admiration, and awe. It has been a privilege participating in their programmes. I have learnt first-hand that mentoring is a two-way learning process, and I continue to be greatly enriched by my association with the organization and the dynamic MEMPROW Girls.

MEMPROW through Ms. Hope Chigudu's[29] eyes

Uganda, Zimbabwe

MEMPROW, AN ORGANISATION A SOUL

POEM

I remember one morning when I discovered a cocoon in the bark of a tree, just as the butterfly was making a hole in its case and preparing to come out. I waited a while, but it was too long appearing, and I was impatient. I bent over it and breathed on it to warm it. I warmed it as quickly as I could, and the miracle began to happen before my eyes, faster than life. The case opened, the butterfly started slowly crawling out, and I shall never forget my horror when I saw how its wings were folded back and crumpled; the wretched butterfly tried with its whole trembling body to unfold them.

Bending over it, I tried to help it with my breath. In vain. It needed to be hatched out patiently, and the unfolding of the wings should be a gradual process in the sun. Now it was too late. My breath had forced the butterfly to appear,

---

[29] Hope Chigudu is an African feminist. She is a Ugandan living in Zimbabwe and is very well known as a gender equality activist and consultant, organisational development expert, and strategist with many African justice groups. She is one of the original Members of MEMPROW's team of resource persons and continues to provide coaching for the staff at MEMPROW.

all crumpled, before its time. It struggled desperately and, a few seconds later, died in the palm of my hand.

Nikos Kazantzakis
Zorba the Greek1

ఛౣఛ

Hatching patiently and grounding the organisation

Grounding forms a foundation and brings clarity. In a state of groundedness, decisions are more easily made, worries about the future are more easily assailed, and enjoyment of the present moment takes on a new lustre and challenge. This is not a state that is detrimental to expanded consciousness but one that enhances it.

MEMPROW grounded itself by taking the time to let its organisational butterfly hatch patiently and unfold its wings gracefully and beautifully. It did not try to grow faster, but it grew organically, very much aware that development cannot be delivered and must be developed.

Hilda Tadria, a founder, rejected all the external support aimed at pressuring the organisation to break out of its cocoon prematurely. She built staff capacity and ensured there were systems,policies, and structures in place before she started fundraising aggressively and exposing the organisation to external pressure. She also ensured that staff was ready to serve the energy of the organisational soul, and that there was authentic empowerment.

Strong stance and values

Right from the beginning, Hilda was clear that a credible women's rights organisation must have a strong stance born out of its clearly articulated values, the heart and soul of what drives it. This stance in the world enables it to engage authentically, assertively, and courageously with both government and donors of every ilk (corporate and non-corporate, national, and international). It enables a vigorous and creative engagement in order to educate, influence, challenge, and share; to say "No" firmly and collegially to donor and other organisations' agendas, while building credibility for itself in the eyes of the world. She, therefore, worked hard to ensure that MEMPROW is defined by strong values and takes the time to immerse staff in those values. Those who do not agree with the values, however, talented, are allowed to leave.

Ideological Clarity and Rooting the Organisation

MEMPROW is not shy about strongly stating its ideological position, whether others agree or resist. It's a feminist organisation and will defend its ideology without backing down, whether a carrot is presented in the form of money or not. Whoever joins the organisation is inducted in feminism. If they are not willing, no matter how talented, sharp, and intelligent, MEMPROW lets them go.

Being ideologically and conceptually clear gives MEMPROW nourishment, power, stability, and growth, because that which has roots will endure and MEMPROW will.

Recruitment of Staff

From the beginning, MEMPROW did not look for people who were well-accomplished and experienced but recruited young, promising people with the capacity and willingness to learn. Hilda and her governance board knew that capacity development requires much more than the transfer of know-how and skills. Other elements such as human relationships, understanding how power operates to either oppress or empower, well-being, and the ability of the organisation to walk alongside young women (its constituency) and give them hope, emerged as being just as important for personal, organisational, and institutional change. From this perspective, MEMPROW has been able to continually focus and respond with flexibility and adaptability to changing circumstances, and to act decisively and with effect in the interests of young women.

Because of what the organisation stands for, it continues to be a magnet for the right talents and hence has the right people in the right roles to enable it to achieve organisational goals.

More of a coach than a leader

Staff might recognize the powerful mission statement but face organisational roadblocks in implementing it. When that happens, the mission statement will only generate frustration and cynicism and decrease motivation among staff members.

From the beginning, Hilda ensured there were no organisational road blocks by acting more as a coach than a leader; coaching in this case means something broader than just the efforts of consultants who are hired to help the organisation build personal and professional skills. The work of consultants is important and vital, but it's executed by outsiders. The coaching being talked about creates a true learning organisation: it is on-going and executed by those inside the organisation; it defines the organisational culture and advances its mission.

Hilda's coaching has unlocked young people's potential as leaders and has contributed to building an organisation that delivers on its purpose. She models the purpose of the organisation by visibly spending her time with staff and the constituency in the field.

Holding a free space

MEMPROW engages in multigenerational dialogues that build on the knowledge and experiences of all kinds of people of different sexualities, age groups, rural and urban, etc., who bring diverse voices that cover issues relevant to young women's rights or who oppose those rights. The dialogues open up conversations that indicate where society is in terms of understanding young women's rights. Some of the regular attendees are feminists who have broken much ground in many fields; space is created for them to share stories of how much it took to get where they are.

What makes the dialogues unique is that MEMPROW holds a free space where contradictions are held; people of different persuasions are allowed to share their contributions. MEMPROW has the inner muscles that enable it to embrace polarities and contradictions that might arise during discussions and has built an organisational form capable of holding them, even without resolution. Clearly, MEMPROW is a thinking organisation that stimulates clear thinking in others.

Leading from the Inside

MEMPROW leads from the inside: ensuring staff members are well equipped, that there is an internal aliveness and creativity that enables them to find new energy and go forward, and does not just respond to the outward; working not only for, but with its constituency. It's like walking alongside instead of in front of someone.

MEMPROW is characterised by a quality of doing that is always self-reflective, critiquing the lenses through which it sees the world, with an emphasis on excellence, practising internally what it is trying to do in the world. Its quality of doing includes being transparent, authentic, and accountable while embracing the principles of personal consciousness, creativity, responsibility, and freedom. This is the quality of doing that changes reality by helping to arouse genuine activism and desire for freedom amongst young people.

Robust collaboration

Common mental attitudes, widespread respect for colleagues' contributions, openness to experimenting with others' ideas, and sensitivity to how one's actions may affect both colleagues' work and the mission outcome are characteristics that one finds in MEMPROW. There is no work that depends entirely on one person; it's always shared responsibility.

MEMPROW also encourages robust collaboration with young and old feminists. It has a pool of resource persons on whom it calls when necessary. Some of these are facilitators, counsellors, yogis, and a range of many others who see themselves as being part of the MEMPROW family.

Creating a Community

Participation in a community is a precondition for true ritual healing, for a sense of belonging that satisfies, for a rewarding understanding of heart, mind, and body connection.

Every time people go into healing retreats or leadership training, at the end there is something like panic. They ask, "How do we keep the intensity we have experienced here while out there?" They fear that the deep sense of community, of connection, they experience in the protected quiet of a retreat or workshop will evaporate shortly after they reintegrate into the world.

The solution perhaps lies elsewhere than in one person showing everyone else the way out. The better answer comes from within. But in order for the answer to emerge from within people, they will need some model that fuels their imagination and creativity.

What MEMPROW does is to create communities for continuity, and as places where young people's individuality is honoured, where their personal gifts can freely be made available to serve the greater good. In these communities, people relate to one another in terms of what each brings to the community, not in terms of how each one appears.

With regard to healing as well as providing support in different ways, MEMPROW creates healing circles: spaces where one is allowed to move, cry, and feel true compassion for other people and for self. The value that one has in a healing community comes from her personal gifts and from the knowledge that she must depend on the personal gifts of others for her own needs to be met. This profound sense of recognition creates a powerful and lasting bond among young people in the healing circle, because they feel heard and seen.

Finishing well

Hilda has finished her work extraordinarily strong as a Director of MEMRPOW and is leaving while still on top. She gave the board time to select and prepare a successor, while trying to ensure the organisation is financially stable.

MEMPROW seen through the eyes of Ms. Maria Alesi[30]

MEMPROW: A Merchant of Hope

"Hope is not a lottery ticket you can sit on the sofa and clutch, feeling lucky. It is an axe you break down doors with in an emergency. Hope should shove you out the door, because it will take everything you have to steer the future away from endless war, from the annihilation of the earth's treasures and the grinding down of the poor and marginal... To hope is to give yourself to the future—and that

---

[30] **Maria Alesi** is a Ugandan feminist and social worker. She is a mentor and resource person within MEMPROW.

commitment to the future is what makes the present inhabitable."

— Rebecca Solnit, *Hope in the Dark*

The transitions of life are more often than not punctuated with complications. From limited information to lack of a present and trustworthy support system, one could argue that a transition can be a nightmare. The confusion, chaos, and anxiety of making the wrong choice. The complete helplessness of having no choices available because the information on choices is either inaccessible or too complicated to get through.

Transitions are even harder when you are young, a sex worker, a woman living under the pangs of patriarchy, or a member of the sexual and gender minority community, to mention a few. In Uganda, being any of these means you come with a mark of oppression hanging over your head. From national laws created to police your existence to socially unsafe spaces posing a threat to your health, livelihood, and associations, the challenges of being a minority both by number and power are the constant hurdles these groups must manoeuvre.

In an environment like this, MEMPROW is what we refer to as the silver lining of the dark cloud. For many young women, men, sexual and gender minorities, sex workers, and other uniquely placed groups, MEMPROW has been and continues to be a safe space, to learn, unlearn, and relearn. A place in which answers to the questions and complexities that punctuate transitions are reached, to save us from the storm's silence on the matters it has raised and continues to raise. MEMPROW has created a unique space for learning, where it convenes persons who are at different points of engaging with gender, patriarchy, and sexuality, while still being able to ensure safe and respectful discussion.

In a world where ageism is rapidly becoming a challenge, the gap between generations is growing quickly and sometimes in an almost toxic manner. MEMPROW, through its intergenerational dialogues, has and continues to do the necessary work to bridge that gap, especially within the feminist movement. The movement is strengthened through enhanced networks and solid alliances. The intergenerational dialogues have enabled different generations of feminists to engage, share experiences, and build sisterhoods based on ideology rather than the difference in age. We all have something to learn from each other.

MEMPROW has also mastered the art of feeding the movement. Through its engagement with young people and students, it has in the past and continues to introduce young women to feminism and create male allies of the movement. The consciousness-raising meetings that happen often not only cover feminism through different lenses and provide space for the young people to learn and strategize, but also to have answers for the critics of their choice to join the movement and identify as feminists. Aside from providing a space for learning, these meetings also create new sisterhoods that support the members on their journey down the road of feminism. This is critical, because identifying as a feminist comes with both joy and a multitude of attacks and sometimes rejection. Through this approach, MEMPROW has played a critical role in building the movement and ensuring sustainability.

The conversation spaces created by MEMPROW are also used to dissect the controversial conversations of the day. The population of Uganda is predominantly religious, with many people including policy-makers using the filter of religion to decide what can and cannot be discussed. However, this has not stopped MEMPROW from providing spaces for learning and frank conversations on women's body rights, sexuality, sexual, reproductive health issues, and sex work.

To be willing and able to take this risk is both a blessing and a curse for MEMPROW. A blessing because these conversations must be had and women need a space to have them—space MEMPROW has created and held for women. A curse because MEMPROW then appears on the radar of those seeking to shut down such discourse. The courage to push the boundaries of the accepted conversations sets MEMPROW as an agent of radical change.

Feminism has for a long time been stereotyped as an elite movement. In Africa specifically, it is looked at as a Western concept. Of course, the word feminism is Western, but the desire and work of women to create an equal world and break free of the patriarchal oppression is not. MEMPROW, through its interaction with women outside of urban areas, has proved this. MEMPROW has been able to simplify the message of feminism and contextualise it to the realities of the women outside of urban areas. Furthermore, MEMPROW has successfully engaged cultural leaders who are the key power holders in the desired change to oppressive traditional practices. Through this, MEMPROW is making the much-needed contribution in consciousness-raising among women and power holders in these areas.

This is particularly important because the majority of women in Uganda and Africa are located in the rural areas. Building movements to push back on patriarchy and other systems of oppression in these areas would mean more women are liberated. This approach also speaks to MEMPROW's ability as an organization to reach a diverse range of women, as it has understood how to navigate class, age, gender, and sexuality while dismantling the systems that create these divides among women.

Movements rely on knowledge to be able to achieve success. MEMPROW is contributing to the knowledge pool for feminism in Uganda. In 2018, they developed a feminist training manual that can be used by organizations and individuals to conduct transformational feminist leadership. The manual provides a simple and contextualised approach to transformational feminist leadership. The manual, which covers the topics of sexuality, economics, solidarity, and ally-ship among others, is a key contribution of MEMPROW to building and sustaining the feminist movement. The manual also shows people that feminism and feminist living is not an airy-fairy theory but a simple collection of daily choices that can radically change and free us.

MEMPROW has provided hope. Hope that the feminist movement, despite the numerous challenges, is still growing. MEMPROW continues to place the axe in the hands of all the people it works with, so they are able to contribute, in all their unique ways, in breaking down the doors of the systems of oppression that keep us bound. With the axe, we cut day by day through the systems of oppression.

❧❧❧❧

Seen through the eyes of Mr. Moses Okwonga[31]

MEMPROW'S achievements in Nebbi, Zombo, and Pakwach Districts and what has made them succeed in their programme

MEMPROW started working in Alur Kingdom at a time when there was a growing concern at the high rate of teenage pregnancy, child marriages, violence against women and girls, and school dropout rates that had negatively affected the sectors of education and health and were likely to undermine any development initiative in the districts that constitute Alur Kingdom, that is: Nebbi, Zombo and Pakwach districts. The major causes of teenage pregnancies and child marriage are attributed to negative cultural practices, low self-esteem, and the breakdown in family systems that leave children to grow up on their own without parental guidance, which consequently impacts on the development of girl children and women, exposing

---

[31] Moses Okwonga is a former Royal Minister of Gender and Youth in Alur Kingdom

them to multiple incidents of violence in the community in which they live.

It should be noted that Alur Kingdom is a patriarchal society, where girls and women are less valued as compared to the men and boys as a result of societal beliefs and practices shaped by environment where girls live. Rural girls and women who come from poor families are deeply affected by gender norms, which determine a girl's future. In order to address the above challenges, MEMPROW partnered with Alur Kingdom and carried out several activities aimed at improving condition of girls and women.

MEMPROW's most important contribution is the support they gave to the Alur King to make pronouncements against negative cultural practices that undermine girls' and women's rights. As a result, King of Alur His Majesty Philip Olarker III, together with all the chiefs, officially denounced Alur cultural practices that devalue women, like the valuing of a boy over a girl child, the prohibition of women from eating nutritious food like eggs and chicken, the practice of forced marriages, and forced widow inheritance.

Many traditional leaders have become ambassadors of change to their subjects, advocating for social norms change. The chiefs are now appointing women in traditional leadership in their chiefdom; for example, in Aryek, Angal, Atyak chiefdoms, twenty percent of their leaders are women, while thirty percent of the Alur Kingdom cabinet are women. Women can now air their views in a traditional court of justice freely without intimidation. The impact of their work is very visible in the entire Kingdom as compared to other NGOs operating in the three districts.

MEMPROW conducted training for cultural, religious, and other duty bearers on GBV laws and government policies on GBV. They also carried out community dialogue meetings in several chiefdoms in which the community were sensitised. As a result, cultural and religious leaders are now reporting a change in social norms, and traditional chiefs have become community champions advancing the rights of women, women controlling resources, and their having access to land and properties. Equally important is their involvement and work with young people who are dynamic and who easily embrace new ideas and change. Over eighty percent of MEMPROW project beneficiaries are young people. Seventy percent of Uganda's population are young people. Therefore, it would be prudent for any wise leader to involve young people, if they want to succeed in their project goals.

Previously, the chiefs and the clan heads handled GBV cases that were criminal in nature in their traditional justice system, with traditional lenses, and they charged an exorbitant sum of money as court fees that local women could not afford. MEMPROW, in their intervention, trained cultural leaders, police, religious leaders, and health workers on laws, policies, and effective referrals of GBV cases. This has seen increased reporting of GBV cases by especially traditional leaders. Traditional leaders are now carrying out mediation of land and GBV cases with feminist consideration. As a result, women's voices are being respected. And there is increased reporting of cases by women to the different existing referral pathways.

There have also been an increased number of women taking up leadership positions in the communities. MEMPROW conducted women's and girls' rights awareness programmes in several schools and chiefdoms in Alur Kingdom. During the sensitisation meeting, women were encouraged to take up leadership positions, because they have the same rights as men and it's their constitutional right.

For example, currently Nebbi district has over thirty LC1 chairpersons who successfully won an election against men. More so, it has given birth to the Nebbi District Women's Forum, where women leaders come together to discuss issues for the betterment of women and girls. The organisation supports community dialogue meetings with community members. The dialogue gave an opportunity to women who rarely had a chance to air their views and concerns on the violence they face in their communities due to social norms. Consequently, it has increased the number of young women and girls standing up for their rights and challenging cultural beliefs and practices that undermine women's and girls' rights.

As part of the MEMPROW intervention in reducing the high rate of teenage pregnancies among young girls, the organisation trained child-mothers in entrepreneurship skills. The purpose was to enable them to acquire business skills for self-sustainability and employment. They were also supported with start-up capital. It was observed that the majority of girls who were victims of early pregnancy are from poor families. The girls are now accessing economic opportunities like Women Entrepreneurship Fund, a youth livelihood programme. Seventy percent of the child mothers who acquired entrepreneurship skills started their own businesses and are now self-employed and able to provide medical and basic needs for their children. As a result, the girls have increased their income levels and as child mothers they have now become agents of change to their peers in their respective communities.

There are several contributory factors to MEMPROW's achievement. Working with existing community structures and relevant government institutions contributed greatly to MEMPROW's success. The organisation worked with the Alur Kingdom structure, LCI & III, police, religious leaders, parents, community champions, health workers, and child-mothers in curbing violence against women and girls. MEMPROW built their capacity and made them understand the magnitude of the issues being addressed. This is intended to bring them in to become part of MEMPROW's team in fighting violence against women and children in the community. This has made MEMPROW's programme gain acceptance and remain sustainable at all levels.

Use of culture in development approach has made MEMPROW's programme gain acceptance by cultural leaders who are custodians of culture and community. The organisation's deep understanding of Alur tradition and culture has caused the community to appreciate and willingly respond to any call to change. Other NGOs often impose what they believe is right without understanding that Alur people love and cherish their culture, which they have lived with for thousands of years. Any call for change should be done with a lot of sensitivity.

The chief of Aryek once made this remark: "MEMPROW doesn't criticize Alur tradition and cultural practices as compared with other NGOs but rather focuses on issues, and we have been able to clearly understand the problem with some of our cultural practices...."

In their training, the MEMPROW team showed a clear understanding of the power dynamics that influence GBV and promote violence against women and girls in the Alur Kingdom. MEMPROW staff understand that unequal power relations are the structural cause of violence against women and girls, because traditional and civic leaders wield power at different levels while taking decisions that affect women and girls. Therefore, MEMPROW's success is attributed to a highly skilled team who are actively involved in challenging and shifting power.

Effective leadership provided by Dr. Hilda Tadria, the Executive Director, significantly impacted on MEMPROW's success on all fronts. She is diversely endowed with enormous knowledge and skill in broad areas of organisational management and operation, richly intertwined with an elaborate acumen of strategic thinking in both spheres of programme development and concrete implementation arrangements to achieve objectives and overall institutional goals. She wields an astute sense of focus in so far as vision and mission are concerned, cherishing the notion of thinking out-of-the-box. Many chiefs in the Kingdom refer to Dr. Tadria as Mama Hilda because of her motherliness. She will forever be remembered in Alur land for having caused social change in the Alur tradition that suppressed women.

She has also built a strong team of committed and dedicated leaders who not only sit in the office to manage but participate in project supervision and support the implementation process. They are able to monitor the implementation process with an eagle eye, identify gaps, and mentor new staff in conducting project activities and ensure adherence to project guidelines. They solicit important information for proposals for fundraising and decision-making.

MEMPROW bases interventions on local evidence. It should be noted that every intervention MEMPROW undertakes is backed by strong evidence analysed by teams of consultants/experts. Over the years, it has been observed that the organisation conducts a baseline survey for every new project to be implemented. This has helped inform proper planning before the execution of a project and adherence to the project life cycle.

MEMPROW seen through the eyes of girls and young women: our primary stakeholders

Girls and young women come to us because they know MEMPROW is a nurturer of girls and young women. They put the mentoring system to the test, and I am glad to say that we passed the test. We have created an organisation that young women relate to and come to; and when asked how they perceived us, this is what they had to say.

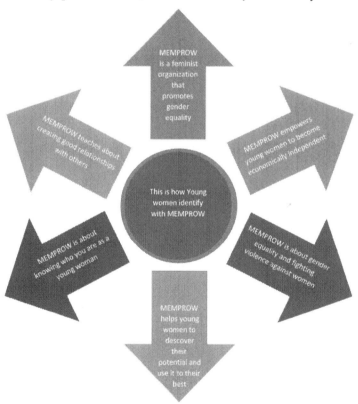

The testimonials below are strong indicators of the organisation's achievement: we have transformed lives in many different ways, but one girl at a time. The mentoring and empowerment approach we have used has changed both mind-sets and behaviour. We have created a community of boys, girls, and young women with purpose for their lives and country; they understand where oppression lies and how to fight back. Each story speaks to these changes.

༺ༀ༺ༀ༺ༀ

Strengthening self-esteem/self-worth, voice, and leadership

Joining MEMPROW and maintaining my position here has been a great joy. Self-esteem was completely low in my entire being before MEMPROW. With MEMPROW, I can now stand in a crowd and speak for myself.

My family was my greatest setback, with no one to believe in me despite my effort and hard work. Everyone believed I did not deserve joy. The words you are told, the names you are called all are a setback.

I kept going forward, for MEMPROW taught me to always look ahead and stop knocking on doors that have already closed. I am great human rights advocate now; I won't look back. Now I am living alone but able to save for my studies and also for my mother's ailment.

—Ajwang Mary Goretti

I did not have self-esteem and the ability to stand and fight for what I deserve and my rights. But with the MEMPROW activities and dialogues, I took part in the Sexual Reproductive and Health Rights. I developed self-esteem and knowledge about protecting my rights, and now I am able to engage in different activities and speak out for myself. I credit MEMPROW for the great work and change it has brought into my life and other girls' lives.

—Kyomugisha Sharon

I was really down; my self-esteem was exceptionally low. This came as a result of my family background; I was raised as the only girl and I had to do almost everything at home while the boys did nothing but watch television. After joining MEMPROW, my life has changed tremendously; I learnt all these life skills through MEMPROW. I can now speak confidently and make my own decisions. Through MEMPROW my leadership skills also greatly improved for example I am the current Public Relations Officer of the MEMPROW girls' network.

ক্যত্যত্য

Strengthening Agency and Voice

How I Met MEMPROW and How It Changed My Life

Like many other young women, Hazra had myriad social and cultural norms stacked against her. Seeing and experiencing violence, oppression, and a stark disparity between men and women created a quest for improving her status quo and that of other young women.

My journey with MEMPROW dates way back when I was in high school, through one of the transformational/mind-blowing programmes dubbed social survival skills training program. I was one of the students who was chosen to attend the two-week programme due to my tenacity and passion for changing the story of many girls. The multi-dimensional programme focused on building my self-esteem and confidence to challenge the patriarchal norms that hinder girls from competing for leadership, and I was no exception. I achieved leadership roles in my institution of learning (school). In addition, this programme gave me knowledge about my body, sexual reproductive health and rights, including menstrual hygiene and HIV/AIDS. Consequently, this intervention shaped my career aspirations and drew me close to the right mentors.

My engagement with MEMPROW not only sparked self-actualisation, but it also offered me training, the right skill sets and mentorship that any young female professional would require to thrive in any part of the world. I honed skills that work across several socio-economic and leadership landscapes. For example, these skills enabled me to compete successfully for a global Commonwealth Scholarship, and I attained a master's degree in Petroleum Economics and Finance in United Kingdom.

From MEMPROW, I also got the opportunity to attend numerous entrepreneurship trainings, such as trainings on business start-ups. Today, I have diversified my resources of income, and I own a successful poultry farm that sustains me and my family. This has exempted me from a challenge that many young women face in trying to access formal employment.

Over the years with MEMPROW, it goes without saying that I have grown into a woman with an underlying passion for the wellbeing of girls and young women.

—Hazra Okem

ৰ্ঙৰ্ঙৰ্ঙৰ্ঙ

I am called Salaama Jaffar at Paida secondary school. My first encounter with MEMPROW was during the social survival skills training.

My life before the training was a mess. I used to not value myself, and I was reckless with life, arrogant and never loved my mum at all. I was violent at home, with plans of leaving school and home. I looked for other ways to get money, which included engaging in intergenerational sex with men.

Along the way, I ended up conceiving and giving birth to a baby girl and went to start a family with the father of my child. At his place, there was a lot of suffering, so I decided to go back home. I was lucky that my parents welcomed me and took me back to school. But still I did not change my life. I embarked on forming bad peer groups who influenced me to start taking alcohol and advised me to leave school. I even contemplated getting married to another man, despite the fact that my baby was eight months then. On the other hand, I also hated my own blood (baby) and left the burden to my mother.

When MEMPROW came to our school, it was a blessing to my life. During the training, we were asked to write bad experiences in our lives and guided accordingly. It was at that point that I realized whatever I was doing was not good and it was risky to my life. That day, when I reached home, I looked into my life, looked at my child, and I felt guilty and shed a lot of tears. I had to make a decision to leave bad company.

I went to my dad and apologized for what I had done. I developed love for myself and looked into my career and realized there was no other person who could make me become what I want to be or meet my goals except me. I had to leave old men whom I was going out with then grab my education and focus.

I am currently obedient at home, exemplary to my young siblings and elders where necessary, and having a good relationship with my mum. I learnt how to deal with stress, left bad peer groups that would influence me to drink, go to discos, and date old men. Today, I love myself and value my education. I recently contested for UNSA general secretary with confidence.

With the difference MEMPROW has had in my life, I was able to bring back my sister, who had left home for prostitution. I managed to talk to her and shared my experience. We are now home with a strong bond with our parents; we love them, value ourselves and our bodies. I am using the knowledge and my experience to sensitize other girls in the community on their behaviours and influence them to stay in school. I stand for no unplanned pregnancies and marriage until when one is done with her studies.

I appreciate MEMPROW for reforming life.

—By Salaama Jaffar

༺༅༅༅

Dapheen's Story of Change

MEMPROW: the mother of many. I do not see her as just an organization but also a home. My first encounter with her was in April 2017, during the Sexual Reproductive Health Rights training at Kampala International University, and my life did not remain the same.

She has groomed me into a young, motivated leader with distinctive needs assessment of young people, a driven desire to impact lives with investment of my personality.

For a young girl from a humble background who was competing with students from well-to do families, wondering how to put my head up, MEMPROW came as an engine to stir me up in all corners of my life. She helped me engage in leadership forums to nurture the leader in me. I started with establishing a club at my University

(KIUMEMPROWSA) that served to fight violence against girls, which was at a peak then.

Irrespective of my humble background with a very touching story, MEMPROW encouraged me to challenge myself to rise above my limitations. She did not allow the strong Dapheen in me to throw in the towel; instead, helping me to fully exercise patience, commitment, dependability, hard work, creativity, innovation, determination, and courage as I shake dust off me to get going.

Through MEMPROW, I was able to get an amazing mentor, Dr. Hilda M. Tadria, who has not only been a friend but also took me on a personal and professional front, as a guardian angel, a mother. She has guided me when my mind was full of questions and dilemmas, and she rescued my pacing soul. The great knowledge and wisdom she has imparted to me has been of great help and support throughout my career. I believe my success is at least in part due to her sincere support and mentorship. She is an excellent friend, teacher, mentor, and a great inspiration to me. She has inspired me to pursue my goals with hard work and dedication.

It is by the MEMPROW fraternity that I was able to complete and attain my first degree. I consider this as a great achievement, because no one in my family (parity six out of eight) had ever attained a degree. I was also the first girl in my village to complete university, when community members were expecting me to drop out of school and get married to one of the hunters in the village.

Through the counselling sessions at MEMPROW, I was able to forgive and love myself like never before. Having grown up in a community with a strong patriarchal set-up that had contributed to my low self-esteem, where girls were seen as less important and a waste of resources, it was a struggle to thrive. The oppressors were all around me, hence the absence of an ear to listen to my trepidations. They would instead judge me and enjoy the blame game. But MEMPROW welcomed me as I was, without any judgement. I have therefore been able to confront my oppressors and tell them I didn't deserve what they did to me and what they do to other girls. MEMPROW has helped the real me come out through self-discovery, impacting lives, and transforming mind-sets through the aptitude to share my story with young people and leading by example. This has happened through the ability to know that I have to live my life to the fullest, because if I don't, no one can live it for me.

MEMPROW has also connected me to different platforms that have been so beneficial in building my career. These platforms include the UN Women mentorship programme, where I got a mentor and an amazing Accountability Partner, who has eased the journey to my growth. MEMPROW has contributed a lot to my current job, where I serve as a social worker. Most skills I use were obtained from attending different dialogues MEMPROW held. This has led to my promotion in less than a year, hence giving me an opportunity and platform to initiate new ideas, like starting up projects and clubs that mentor and empower young girls and refugees.

I have learned to own my story and work on being a better version of me in pursuit of my ability to inspire, change and impact lives, to live to fullest, and to leave a legacy.

LONG LIVE MEMPROW!

—Dapheen Kemigisha

ক্ষ-ক্ষ-ক্ষ-ক্ষ

Expanding horizons and aspirations

Going to New York was a reality that had never been in my dreams. You know how you get up one morning and you have a flight that evening, but you feel like everything is just a mirage? Yet it should have been a déjà vu, and after all this occurs, you actually get to believe, "Okay, now this is real, this is actually happening to me right now!" You imagine the extreme joy and slight fear at that exact time, right? Now yeah, that's what it felt like. I visited New York for a week to attend a leadership retreat formed by an organisation known as Miracle Corners of the World (MCW). It was themed "Local Change through Global Exchange."

On this retreat, we were only youth but from different parts of the world, and we had the opportunity to share our stories and experiences. We were helped to come up with a vision inspired by the person you are or what you have been through, and also from the perspective of the change you want to see in your society or where you come from. I went as a MEMPROW Girl, and I'm proud to say I was the only representative from Uganda in 2015. It was a delightful and, at the same time, soothing experience, I must say. It's astonishing how people from different parts of the world have similar stories and experiences, especially on issues regarding gender-based violence, war, and conflict, but also similar achievements. These differences and similarities in our various walks of life formed a bond between us, so we could embrace and understand one another better. There would come a point when we'd all laugh out loud and a point when we'd all break down and cry. But this only helped us become better people/leaders.

I learned that it's actually rude to judge people without knowing who they are or what their perception of life is. In addition, I also learned that, as a leader, one has to be tolerant, accepting, and understanding; these three aspects are the main ingredients of humanity. If our social habits are embedded with a high percentage of humanity, unity becomes inevitable. Until next time.

I vividly remember the first time I encountered MEMPROW. It was in 2012, when they held a social survival skills training at my school, Nabisunsa Girls' School, and I was lucky to be chosen among the participants. We were about thirty-five girls in a room, and it was the first day to participate in the social survival skills training. I was neither scared nor bothered, just a little tensed up—you know, when you do not know what to expect but are ready and open to whatever comes.

Then we had different facilitators throughout the week telling us about sexual reproductive health and the rights that come along with it; patriarchy (that was the first time I heard about this word in my life, and since then it has never left my vocabulary); confidence-building; etiquette; social structure and gender equality, among others.

Before MEMPROW, I was extremely ignorant, and the thing with ignorance is that it's too blissful. You never notice you are ignorant or whether it's a bad thing until you are informed and knowledgeable. You think that whatever is just is, and there is nothing you can do about it; and our natives just tell you to merely pray about it. You pray, pray, and pray until you don't even know what you are praying for, why you are praying, or whether it's even working. So you just remain there, ignorant but happy, because ignorance is exactly that—*bliss*. Now that was me without doubt.

I was mindless, less aware, and ignorant about the things that happened around me and also about the intensity of the challenges that girls and women at large go through. One morning, two of the MEMPROW team members told us to walk while they observed us; they kept on commenting as to who walked "well" and who didn't. In my head, I was thinking, "Why the hell are they really judging how we walk?" But as a student, I hung in, laughing at people who did not perform according to the standards set by the two MEMPROW staff members.

These two ladies walked one after the other; head held high, back straight, chest in position, one foot following its partner without dragging. We all clapped immediately, and from then onwards we called that the "MEMPROW Walk." Up to date, if I come across a girl/lady walking with a bowed head, her shoulder falling, and her shoes dragging, my mind goes, "Clearly she isn't a MEMPROW girl." If it is in my capacity, I reach her and bring her up to speed. If it's not, I let it slide, hoping that one day she will learn she has to walk like she owns the place. One can only, or mostly, let empowerment in through a door opened by oneself.

The social survival Skills Training taught me things I would never learn in school, because they were never taught. In school, you learn to read, cram, and reproduce it on an examination paper to validate that you crammed well and performed well. But as soon as you are out, you forget everything. Don't get me wrong: I believe in and love education. I just have a few issues with a portion of the school setting, but that's a story for another day.

This training was very impactful to me and my life; my mind-set about the status quo changed completely. I learned to live and not just merely stay alive. I learnt to live with purpose, to have purpose, and I got to know that schooling is not final, one has to learn social survival skills. I have learned to be aware and more alert about the happenings in my community, country, and world at large. I have made friends with empowered girls and women, which has helped me shape a positive attitude towards life.

I participated and engaged in various civil servant activities like debates and leadership trainings, and I have written women empowering poems, one of which got me to be a mentee at the local change for global exchange program in the USA. I have learned to empower other girls and women; I have helped my community members and become a better listener. I am currently a cofounder of Kitara Nation, a poetry organization based in Uganda that trains students to do poetry, uses page poetry, performance poetry, and theatre poetry for entertainment.

I have developed a firm positive attitude towards life, and it has helped me never to give up in whatever I set out to do, like Kitara Nation and the active Debate Society of Uganda, where I am a member. I encourage my brothers to be good people, inform them of the formalities of patriarchy in our society, and urge them to ensure they dismantle or contribute to its dismantling. I empower the girls in my community, teach them to write CVs, encourage them to finish school, and often to come for the MEMPROW dialogues held monthly—never do they regret it.

I never look back; I have attended most of the trainings organized by MEMPROW. I have invited many people to it and have started conversations and engaged in discussions about the dismantling of patriarchy. Prayer only works with hard work. I no longer just pray and pray ignorantly. I pray only for something I'm already working towards. After MEMPROW, I should say Empowerment resides in me and information has an uncontrollably high affinity for me. If the position existed, I could be a MEMPROW Ambassador right now. I am proud to be associated with MEMPROW and more than glad to be a "MEMPROW gal."

—Hawa Nanjobe Kimbugwe

కోకోకోకో

Reclaiming personal identity and self-worth

Joining MEMPROW was a game changer for me. I always felt like something was lacking in my life and always looked out for that one thing that completed me. I kept complaining to myself about my physical appearance and this made me feel incomplete. As a result, I always felt shy to speak in public since I feared that people would start describing my physical appearance while others would quote the mistakes in my speech. Because of low self-esteem, I always wanted the ground to swallow me up. All this held back my abilities. When I first joined MEMPROW in 2016, I was so conservative with poor communication skills and knew little about what life meant. The MEMPROW girls tried to mentor me and I also attended the social survival skills training where I learnt that no one is perfect in all aspects of life; each and every one of us in the world have their flaws. I also learnt that communication is the heart of living and that if you want to live a good life, you must learn how to communicate. I learnt to be responsible for my own happiness.

All this has changed my life; I got to know the facts of life. I am now glad and proud of the person I have become. No one can ever criticize me again because of my physical appearance; I appreciate the person I am. I realized the leader in me; I am currently a disciplinary prefect at school. I now stand my grounds and associate with people of all kinds, characters and origin without having difficulty. This transformation was because of MEMPROW and I trust that this was an opportunity for a lifetime. And I wish that each and every girl who is in this country gets such an opportunity. The world will be better place to live in.

Long Live MEMPROW!

—Nakato Jazzira

≈ତ≈ତ≈ତ≈ତ

Unleashing passion for women's rights activism and personal independence

I joined MEMPROW in 2011, when I was still at Bishop Cipriano Kihangire Secondary School in form five. I received an invitation from my sister (Sally), who by then was at the university and an active MEMPROW girl. The trainings were still being conducted at the Imperial Royale Hotel in Kampala. My first training was on social etiquette, and for sure, my first encounter with MEMPROW left me with a very huge desire to continue attending all MEMPROW activities, since it exposed me to quite a big number of people whom I had always longed to meet in life.

Before I joined MEMPROW, I was an extremely shy girl with a low voice tone, and much as I had always desired to be a great public speaker, this seemed like a dream that would never come true. Even in the struggle to become one, I tried joining the debaters' and writers' club at my school but only ended up in positions that would not require me to talk, like the treasurer. But when I joined MEMPROW, it was like an "eye opener" for all my dreams.

At MEMPROW, I found so many young girls who were very audible and eloquent speakers and extremely confident, along with the fact that MEMPROW gave us free space where we were allowed to say whatever we wanted to say regardless of our age, status, tribe, and age. My confidence was boosted, and I gained morale to start expressing myself freely in the public. First of all, I have gained confidence and also learnt how to be audible when speaking. I am glad people are always telling me after every presentation that I am really a great presenter. I have mostly evidenced this in my MBA class at MUBS and at Network for Active Citizens, where I am currently working.

I have gained knowledge on gender and feminism, and I am really glad to say proudly that I am a feminist, and this has become part of me in all my spaces. Most people keep calling me names being tagged on feminists, like the bold one. At my undergraduate program, I encouraged so many girls from Makerere University to join MEMPROW, and I even created a MEMPROW WhatsApp group that is now being used by the MEMPROW staff members to communicate all the upcoming activities. I have also helped many of my friends to be more assertive, especially those who were facing intimate partner violence.

I have learnt to strongly protect and advocate for women's rights to an extent that I have even become a very strong advocate for gender equality. This is evidenced by the fact that most of my social media platforms are always advocating for that. I have taken this to even the national level, where I always use the gender lens in analysing the national budget, and I advocate for fair allocation of issues that strongly affect women, like the SRHR Services.

As a way of replicating what MEMPROW taught me, I have dedicated myself to do the following at both the family level and the community level, as indicated below.

* **Self/Personal development:** I have been able to start my personal business, and this has enabled me to

subsidize the little earnings I get from the place where I work.

* **At Family level:** I have taught my brothers to learn how to embrace women as normal human beings, and therefore they have learnt to help in the house chores, compared to before, when they used to leave all the house chores to the girls.

* **At Community level:** I have taught the adolescent girls and young women to make reusable sanitary towels, and in so doing I have been able to enhance their knowledge to promote menstruation hygiene management. This has demystified the process and cycle of menstruation among girls.

—By Nanyonjo Cathy

৯৯৯৯

Boys, too, have joined MEMPROW to champion the rights of girls

My first encounter with MEMPROW was at Luzira S.S in 2015. I was invited by a friend, and I was changed positively by the article of Dr. Tadria in the newsletter of 2015. I lacked the knowledge of living positively and peacefully with girls both at home and at school, i.e., I had a negative attitude towards girls.

I used to disrespect and bully girls both at home and at school. I always thought boys were not supposed to do housework, and I used to leave such work to my sister at home. However, after my encounter with MEMPROW, all these are no more. I now engage in doing housework and fight in my capacity to see that girls are respected and given their rights and freedom. I cannot, for example, just see a girl at school in tears and fail to find out the cause, because it torments me.

I have gained a positive attitude and respect for girls and have learnt to live and mix freely and happily with them. I have learnt that I have a part to play in promoting girls' education and rights, and I have gained counselling skills. I am also the MEMPROW Club boy's coordinator at my school. I have lost some of my male family members, who are still biased about women and think I have sold out on men, but I still encourage them to promote their girl children's' education and to end violence

On personal level, I have been creative by finding positive ways of economically sustaining myself and family. At family and community level, I spread the gospel and knowledge at home, and the boys now treat girls fairly.

Thank you, MEMPROW, because I wouldn't be the good person I am today if MEMPROW hadn't come to my school.

—Ssenkubuye Anthony Woods

ঙঙঙ

Claiming a right to violence-free relationships and environments

My first encounter with MEMPROW Uganda was during a five-day training held at Makerere University in my second year, which was academic year 2013/2014. Before joining MEMPROW, I had a different mind-set.

However, MEMPROW gave me an opportunity to unlearn and relearn. Below are a few things that described my life:

I was timid and didn't believe in myself or my capabilities. I thought I had to depend on my then-boyfriend for my success, as he was highly successful. My mind-set in regards to sexual orientation and gender roles was solely based on being either female or male in a patriarchal society. Before joining MEMPROW, I was in a relationship that I found exciting and cool. However, after the MEMPROW training in 2014, I understood what Gender-Based Violence was. I didn't know what constituted Gender-Based Violence and abusive relationships.

Currently, I believe in myself and don't need to depend on someone for my survival or success. I am more open-minded and more understanding when it comes to sexual orientation. I can easily identify cases of GBV and abusive relationships. After the training, it took me some time, although I later got the courage to get out of my physically and emotionally abusive relationship. I was able to gain courage to defend a friend who was being hit by her boyfriend. It took a lot of courage, as his friends were threatening to beat me up.

Before I joined MEMPROW, I was in a relationship that I found pretty nice and cool. When I went for the MEMPROW training, they explained abusive relationships and Gender-Based Violence. I thought that I needed him to succeed and, without his assistance, my chances to live a great life were limited. He had convinced me to quit my job and that he would take care of me, since he would be paying me more than any employment at the time. I did an assessment and realized I was in an abusive relationship that needed to end. I also had a meeting with Dr. Tadria, who advised me that my dreams as an individual are valid, and I needed to respect myself enough to choose my aspiration. After the realization that my relationship was not getting any better, I decided to end it.

It took me some time though, as I continued to train with MEMPROW until 2017, when I finally ended it. It was a tough decision that I only made when I got to the realization that the situation I was in was not about to change. It was quite painful, as I was at a point when I was scared for my own life and survival. My life now is way better. I realized my value and the dream I wanted to pursue. I looked for jobs and got employed; I am currently employed with the bank.

I have learnt to be more understanding and open-minded. During discussions, I encourage people to think out of the box and be more objective in their thought process. I am a counsellor at my church, and my focus is to assist people to discover who they are.

I have reworked my life and realized my success doesn't depend on anyone but myself. I am now employed and pursuing my post-graduate degree at Uganda Management Institute. I am currently pursuing my post-graduate degree from the Chartered Institute of Marketing. I also got accepted to one of the top universities, the London School of Economics & Political Science (LSE), to pursue my master's degree. My career is pivoting towards my desired direction. Yes, the sky is only the beginning.

—By Lillian Kansiime

≼ᓫ≼ᓫ≼ᓫ≼ᓫ

When I joined MEMPROW, I did not know about sexual reproductive health rights and different contraceptives. I also didn't know about how to start up a business. Upon joining, I acquired skills of how to start a business; I have become more confident about myself despite all the gender stereotypes that undermine women in our societies. I speak out in cases of sexual harassment and violations of other women's rights. I share this with people in my community, advocating on social media among other things, discouraging bad cultural practices that cause harm to women.

MEMPROW increased my self-reliance. At first, I didn't believe so much in myself. But when I attended MEMPROW's training, it shaped my mind-set. I became more confident; I aimed for leadership positions, which created a platform for me to advocate for the rights of women. I contested with two boys for president of the social work association at KIU; I was the only girl who went for that post. I was able to make it, and the same semester I went for guild elections. In each college, they wanted four representatives; there were seven candidates (two girls and five boys). I was the third in the first four and the only girl to go through in the college. Because of the confidence I had, I was appointed as the minister of gender and social affairs of KIU main campus. Besides that, I was also given other responsibilities in other associations.

My passion is to serve humanity and create a positive impact in my life, family, community, nation, and the whole world. I give great thanks to MEMPROW!

—By Hasahya Sovereign

Why and how have we been successful in building a community of empowered girls and women?

We defined a transformative mentoring and mind-set change couched in a feminist and human rights framework. Change came about when girls and women, as well as boys and men, understood the root causes of gender inequality and the universality of human rights. There is a powerful awakening when young women realise they are not less equal, and they understand that hierarchy and subordination is the status quo in patriarchal systems affecting all women. In the social survival training programmes, we maintained our focus on adolescent girls and young women between the ages of thirteen and twenty-nine. In this way, we were able to ensure that the content remained relevant to their lives.

The examples of the content include topics such as personal empowerment and social intelligence; understanding and managing peer pressure; effective communication and negotiation; patriarchy and gender identity; understanding and dealing with sexual gender-based violence; as well as their sexual reproductive health and rights. The training included career planning and discussions on responsible citizenship. We introduced professional writing skills, so the girls and young women can tell their stories, and we provided sustained mentoring thorough intergenerational gender dialogues and personal counselling.

The result of this work is that MEMPROW has a strong constituency, a power base that can be used by other activists who want to engage with young people, especially those in schools and tertiary institutions. It has paved the way in some of the poorest districts and hence opened doors for others to follow. It provides a unique perspective on contemporary Uganda and the situation of young women, while awakening their awareness to discrimination and inequality, as the testimonies above have shown. It is a fact that when organisations are looking for confident young women to speak out, MEMPROW is the organisation to go to.

My contributions through MEMPROW's work have gone beyond empowering girls to transforming young men's negative mind-sets and those of communities within which girls and women work. We decided to introduce our stakeholders at the community level to concepts of gender and human rights as a strong base for practicing innovative new forms of power and leadership, in a way that encourages collective power, because individualistic patriarchal power is neither good for men and communities nor for women. As a result of this work, some communities have realised that, working together, they can form a strong movement capable of protecting girls and young women and providing access to justice and rights. The following testimony from one of our male stakeholders is evidence to this.

৶৶৶৶

I was introduced to MEMPROW by a friend and a co-worker in early 2009, when he invited me. We had shared a lot about making a significant impact in the lives of young people in Uganda, after personally having seen the suffering of children and girls while I traversed several hard-to-reach corners of this beautiful country as a research assistant. After attending a couple of MEMPROW intergenerational mentoring and gender dialogue network monthly sessions, I felt ready to follow my dream of reaching out to young people.

My best lesson at MEMPROW turned out to be my turning point. I vividly remember when Dr. Hilda reached out to me as one of the few men who were in attendance and asked me, and I quote, "Yes, Charles, how are you? How do you always manage to make it to the monthly dialogue meetings without fail?"

And I answered, "Doctor, I am a man. I manage."

Her reply changed me forever when she said, "That is the reason why you are here. We want to change your mind-set, if you think women cannot manage doing what you are doing."

Indeed, my mind-set was changed after taking the training on gender and patriarchy, feminist value clarification, human rights, negotiations in relationships, among others.

᯽᯽᯽᯽

Community Development and Strengthening Women's Agency

My life-changing work was not limited to working with girls only. I started working as an activist for women's agency in my teenage years when my mother requested me to teach reading and writing to the women in the community women's groups she had formed to train them in reproductive health, family hygiene, and nutrition.

At the time, talking about women's rights was looked at with disdain. My mother, an activist herself, would not be silenced on rights. But even for her, she could not talk about sexual reproductive health rights. I once asked her why we never brought discussions on family planning in the group discussions.

"I have eleven children," she said. "Who would listen to me?" Instead, she opted to have small groups of women in the community where women would meet to talk about their experiences.

What stood out for me were the stories exchanged among women of how they managed to deal with the oppressive patriarchal power and how they stood up and exercised their agency. When some of them expressed fear that their husbands might stop them from coming to the group meetings, my innovative mother suggested that the discussions include lessons in hygiene, reading, and writing. Her argument was that no reasonable person would stop a woman, in whose hands the family health rested, from attending training on health, reading, and writing.

That is how I was brought into the community development work. It became my sole responsibility to teach them how to read and write. Most of the women had never been to school, so they did not read or write. Their desire was to learn how to write their name and read letters written to them by their children or to read the Bible and church hymns for themselves. My toughest experience during that time was getting the women to hold a pencil. Their hands and fingers had become so stiff with work that they could not bend around a pencil. This reality hit me so hard, but it also became a point for light moments with laughter as we organised competitions on who could hold the pencil best. When one has the benefit of an education with nimble fingers, it is difficult to understand how liberating the ability to hold a pencil and write one's name is.

Working with my mother, I understood the importance of the "do no harm" principle that has become "NGO-ised," sometimes just to tick the box of donor requirement. I began to appreciate why she was incredibly careful to send the women back home with products of their labour, such as cakes baked during the session. I learned that this was to minimise the chances of domestic violence from men who were not happy that their wives went to the women's clubs, as they were known then.

My mother encouraged women to practise what they learned, but she also reminded them to be keenly observant and report back any learning that could have put them in danger. When such a case was reported, she would make a point of going to that home to talk to the husband. Once, we nearly caused harm to a woman whom I will call Joyce for ease of reference. Joyce reported to us how she narrowly survived a beating by her husband, after putting into practice what she'd learned that day.

She had gone home after a day of learning about hygiene, very anxious to prove that all was good. That day, we had talked about water-borne diseases and their harm in the community, when the people drink non-boiled water. Most people knew this, and they did not drink water, so in our lesson of the day, we emphasised the importance of boiling and drinking water for health. Joyce went home and boiled water for the family.

In my Bakiga culture, it was not accepted to present a drink to a husband in any container. A reputable woman, my mother included, had a special container, a gourd, in which they presented a special non-alcoholic drink made from sorghum to the husband. Generally, this is why, in Bakiga homes, water was not respected as a drink. Presenting water as a drink implied the women in the house had not bothered to make the porridge.

Joyce, to impress her husband about her newly acquired knowledge, prepared a good dinner to soften the ground for acceptance of drinking water. She then brought a gourd that she normally presented with the traditional drink, but this time full of clean boiled water, and presented it to her husband. Thinking it was the usual drink, Bushera, which is still a favourite among Bakiga even today, he took a big sip and quickly spat it out.

Joyce narrated the story, telling of how she had not seen her husband shout at and abuse her since becoming a committed Christian, adding that it was his new Christian faith that saved her from a beating. To make up for this, my mother ordered that I cook an appeasement meal, which we carried to Joyce's home. This gave us an opportunity to talk to her husband. We were able to bring him to accept drinking boiled water, especially given that making sorghum porridge is very labour-intensive. I learnt then that one can cause harm even when good is the goal. But I also learned that one must be deliberate in undoing the harm caused.

With time, my mother was able to convince the then-Ministry of Culture to include her voluntary work under the Government's Community Development Programme, and she was credited for bringing health and economic development to many homes. At her funeral, a woman who spoke on behalf of all the women in her community talked of how Justine, my mother, brought value and dignity to women. I smiled because we had been partners in this agenda.

Bringing change beyond national boundaries

My contribution to fighting for gender equality and women's rights beyond local communities first came with the opportunity to join the Eastern and Southern African Management Institute. Created by the East Africa Community, it expanded beyond the region. In 1980, it was established as an intergovernmental regional management development centre to service the eastern and southern African countries.

In 1997, through a resolution of the Council of Ministers, the United Nations Economic Commission for Africa (UNECA) designated ESAMI as a centre of Excellence for Management Development in Africa. True to Excellence, it was among the few, if not the first, regional organisations to establish a full programme on Women in Development. This is the programme I was recruited into in 1986. The focus was to train middle to senior managers from the region to improve their managerial performance, taking into consideration the global issues but with a regional focus relevant to the African environment.

It is because of this that I was able, together with my colleague, Misrak Elias, to work with and strengthen agency of women from all over the region. Through this work, we brought women's value in the workplace to centre stage. We met many women whose workplaces had normalised exclusion and accepted gender-role stereotyping and role allocation; where women's access to work entitlements were honoured or dishonoured on the basis of patriarchal gender norms. Many years after I left the organisation, I continued to get messages from the women we had trained, expressing appreciation for having given them a voice and brought them dignity in the workplace.

The years I worked at the Economic Commission for Africa, from 1997 to 2007, as a Regional Advisor on Women's Economic Empowerment, were the peak of my public service in working for gender equity and equality.[32] I

---

[32] "Gender equality" means equal outcomes for women, men, and gender-diverse people. "Gender equity" is the process to achieve gender equality. Approaches to achieving gender equity recognises that women and gender-diverse people are not in the same "starting position" as men and that gender equity measures are needed to level the playing field.

moved my professional interventions upstream and focused on integrating gender issues in national policies and training top government officials in gender-responsive planning and policy formulation. I am proud that I was the architect of the first gender policies in several countries, including one in my country, Uganda, where I led the process of drafting the first National Gender Policy (NGP), which was finally approved in 1997. At a time when gender mainstreaming was little known and suspect, I was among the front runners in moving policy planning from a practical need focused planning for women to a strategic planning for women[33] in many African countries. Gender mainstreaming as a planning tool has had its critiques. But when effectively used with appropriate gender analysis tools, it focuses planning on the intersectionality of women's lives. This is the work I am known for on the African continent.

I believe the icing on the cake in my career is my contribution to levelling the resource mobilisation and redistribution playing field for women in Africa, through

---

This gender equity planning is achieved thorough gender analysis, a tool of social economic and political analysis through women's perspective.

[33] Caroline Moser's distinction between practical needs and strategic needs introduced a powerful tool of gender analysis that strengthened gender-responsive policy planning. Practical needs are ones that, if met, help women in current activities and may entrench women in their situation of subordination to patriarchal norms. Strategic needs are needs that, if met, give women agency and transform the balance of power between men and women.

the creation of the African Women's Development Fund[34] that I co-founded together with Bisi Adeleyi Fayemi and Joan Forster (RIP). I have already talked about how this happened as a result of feminist rage caused by a realisation that women in Africa could not organise a decent regional meeting due to a lack of resources. Meeting with two strong African feminists from different countries and setting up an organisation that serves women on the whole continent challenges the negative perception that women cannot work together and be successful.

Today, AWDF is very competently managed by a team of all African women for African women. Since 2001, AWDF has stayed true to its core goal: to build up an autonomous base for gender equality and development, supporting movements and initiatives of women that ordinarily do not have access to mainstream sources of funding for reasons of capacity, language, geographical location, and marginalisation.

Since its formalisation in the year 2000, at the time of writing this book, AWDF has awarded grants of US$48.7 million to over 1,300 women's organisations in forty-six

---

[34] The African Women's Development Fund (AWDF) is a grant-making foundation that supports local, national, and regional women's organisations working towards the empowerment of African women and the promotion and realisation of their rights. By specialising in grant-making and focused, tailored movement-building programmes, we work to strengthen and support the work of African women's organisations. By amplifying and celebrating African women's voices and achievements, AWDF supports efforts that combat harmful stereotypes and promote African women as active agents of change.

countries in Africa and the Middle East. AWDF has developed a unique, flexible, and responsive approach to grant-making. This approach has catalysed change in the lives of women, particularly those from marginalised communities, and at the levels of policy (https://awdf.org/impact/). I pay tribute to all the women at AWDF, who have continued to hold the dream of three African women from Ghana, Nigeria, and Uganda and made it a truly African Women's Dream.

I exited formal public service in 2020, a landmark year in which the world temporarily closed down. After this, when the world opens, it will never be the same, not just because of my retirement, but mainly because of COVID-19. Social relations will change in ways we have not known them, because of social distancing, a concept that has taken long to internalise, especially in Africa, even when we were told it is a lifesaver. Hopefully, because of the lesson we will have learned from the pandemic: that we are all human and equal.

But more fundamentally, the pandemic has opened a window into what have been women's ignored experiences. Jessica Horn,[35] the then Programme Manager, put it so clearly while writing on impacts of CODIV-19:

---

[35] Jessica Horn: "Surviving COVID19: Why we need to listen to African women's Organisations." https://medium.com/@AWDF/surviving-covid19-why-we-need-to-listen-to-african-womens-organisations.

"Generalised catastrophe may well be the 'new normal' for the privileged, but it has been the backdrop of African women's organisations for generations. In the two decades of the African Women's Development Fund's operations, our grantees have worked to try to get one step ahead of epidemics such as HIV/AIDS and Ebola, to mobilise to end war in their countries and communities, and to pick up the social, political, and economic pieces in its aftermath. Beyond headline disasters, grantees have also worked persistently on the quieter but no less deadly threats of economic collapse and everyday economic precarity, and the reality that the patriarchal violence against us as women costs us our emotional and economic wellbeing, and sometimes also costs us our lives. So, it is not surprising that as COVID19 started to touch the continent, AWDF grantees were already outlining a political agenda for the response, warning of possible consequences if we fail to be attentive to the fact that health crises are always gendered."

2020 will forever be known as the year when difference in sex, colour, class of whatever kind, or geography did not count. But difference in gender did continue to matter, as women became victims of increased violence and some had to sleep in markets during the lockdown, as in the case of market women in Uganda, to make sure their children did not go hungry.

CHAPTER SEVEN

MY GOLDEN PRINCIPLES FOR LIFE

"We are staring down the line at the single biggest transition of power and leadership our workplaces and society have ever witnessed. In light of this, it is more important than ever that leaders are taking steps to ensure that the lessons they have learned throughout their careers can be passed on to the next generation. A failure to do so would be as professionally reckless as it would be tragic."

—Michael McQueen[36]

I AM USUALLY ASKED where I, in my mid-seventies, get my energy to be doing the work I am doing. Also, do I ever plan to retire? In this chapter, I want to share what I call my Golden Principles or my DNA, as Michael McQueen calls it, which make me tick.

---

[36] Michael McQueen: "What is Your Leadership DNA? How to distil the foundations of your success and life." In his essay, McQueen describes leadership DNA as the three elements of every leader's character DNA: Defining Experiences, Non-Negotiable, and Values: Axioms for Living and Leading.

Defining Experiences

My experience of the power of patriarchy has defined my feminism, which in turn has defined how I have lived for most my life; it defines my feminist rage and produces energy of its own to deal with inequality. Today, I look everywhere for inequality, especially racial and gender, in every action and statement.

I have heard many women say they will not take feminism into their homes; that to maintain peace in their homes, it has to be left at the gate. I regard this as maintaining peace at all costs. When you leave your feminist principles at the gate, you are denying your rights to equal treatment, a voice, and a right to say no to violence.

There is no time to retire from the feminist agenda and work of fighting for women's rights, because if any one of us snoozes, we lose. We may not always be successful, but as Winston Churchill once said, "Success is not final, failure is not fatal—it is the courage to continue that counts." I tell myself, when I retire from feminist work, it will be because I am dead, because feminism defines my thoughts, my choices, and my dreams of a different world for us women and girls; a better world where women do not have to tiptoe around men or package ourselves for approval of who we are as women.

My defining feminist experience was watching my mother fight against patriarchy the whole of her life, starting from when she was forced into a marriage at sixteen years of age, on her holidays from school; sometimes winning and sometimes losing, but always transforming losses into gains.

When my daughter was much younger, she used to tell me I was exaggerating barriers to gender inequality. My experiences defined the way I saw the world, always through women's struggles against patriarchal oppression. She, on the other hand, saw the world differently. She grew up in a home where there were no gender assigned roles; she had a father who washed dishes, cooked, and cleaned house, and a mother who led a public life, so she saw the world in the narrow world of her family. Then she got married and joined the workforce. Several years later, she wrote me an email one day starting with, *Dear Mama, I am a latecomer to feminism.* At that moment, my cup was full because my daughter had become fully conscious of oppression and could no longer be a bystander.

Many young women are quick to excuse themselves from taking a feminist stand because they have taken the gains of women's rights for granted. Many of them do not understand how feminist advocacy enabled women to make inroads into the Ugandan Parliament, where we now have a one-third female membership, and they are beginning to question affirmative action principles put in place to address gender gaps and inequalities. University girls who have made it to this institution of higher learning express embarrassment when they learn they were able to get to University because of the affirmative action policies fought hard for by women in Uganda to increase women's participation in the University and higher education. My advice to young people is, find your defining moment and use it to move on.

Define your aspirations high but live within your means

"Fear of not measuring up runs very deep. That is because we tend to live competitively instead of creatively. Competitiveness makes us lose not only our flow of inspiration, but even our courage and conviction, too, and so we end up destroying our unique and precious gifts and talents by comparing them with others."[37]

When I was growing up, I never understood how my parents got enough money to pay for a full education for all of their eleven children. Thankfully, I grew up to understand that my father's mantra of "Oteine Teitwa" (no one can kill you for what you do not have) was his way of telling us to live within our means. What has this meant for me? Today, I know this has shaped and continues to shape the way I live. It means I am under no stress for competition with anyone. I will not borrow to buy something just because, someone has it or it is in fashion.

But living within one's means goes beyond financial decisions; it also means accepting and loving who you are. When I started losing my hair, I went all over buying wigs, good ones that cost a lot of money, but they were also very uncomfortable in our tropical weather. I realised I was

---

[37] *Gardening the Soul, A Spiritual Day Book Through Seasons* by Sister Stanislaus Kennedy. New York: Simon & Schuster, Ltd. 2001.

falling into the trap of an inability to accept what I look like and decided to give up the wigs and cut off the remainder of my hair. Today I meet people who automatically assume I am a cancer survivor or a crazy feminist. Total strangers stop me and want to have a conversation about my hairless head. One young woman once told me I am not a good Christian. I have learned to live within the means of what I look like.

This is one principle I have had to bring into the training with young girls and young women who have difficulty accepting what they look like. But this inability to accept what they look like, for women in general, is also embedded in patriarchal definitions of a woman. The idea that a woman's beauty is defined by long, straight hair, if you are black, or beautiful legs (whatever that means). In many of our black cultures, light-coloured skin is still internalised as a sign of beauty by both men and women at an early age. This determines the extent to which we spend so much money that could be put to better use, beautifying ourselves with dangerous lightening cream.

In our work with girls, we found that their perceptions of having failed to meet the social (patriarchal) standards of beauty are one of the causes of their negative self-worth. We have met girls with long legs, short legs, thin legs, and big legs all saying they hate their legs. Negative self-worth among girls, we learned, is commonly caused by the belief that they do not have beautiful legs, hair, or a light skin colour. So, the training focuses on getting them to accept and appreciate what they look like. This is always our starting point, helping them to learn to accept what they look like. The world takes on a new, exciting challenge, and when you accept to live within the means of what you have or look like.

Axioms for Living and Leading

These axioms summarize various mentalities and assumptions that have guided the ways I view myself and the world around me.

People often ask me how I have been able to balance a life as an international civil servant and global consultant with being a wife and mother as well as daughter, plus a feminist warrior, and still maintain sanity. Where do I get the courage and energy to continue? Sometimes I also ask myself the same question, where do I get the courage under challenges of personal loss or failures?

My core mentality and reaction is to always look for the silver lining in whatever is happening in my life. Over time, this has consistently given me courage, resilience, and then ability to move on.

People told me I was strong when I lost my husband simply because I was not wailing and throwing myself down in misery, and when I returned back to work within three weeks. I told myself they do not know how I am feeling inside, with a stomach churning and a chest so constricted that sometimes I could not breathe. No one could see this, so they did not know. They did not know I was so shaken, I feared being in public places after the funeral; I needed my son to accompany me to the banks and the supermarkets, because I had no strength to face these places alone. We always did things together with my husband. We walked together and sat together wherever we went. In Rotary, where we both belonged, we were known as love birds. So how have I endured some real-life challenges and emerged with sanity?

I believe I have been able to endure shock because I am always looking for a silver lining in all the ugly experiences. Second, I believe very strongly that, if I allow myself to wallow in misery and be stuck looking back, I will become a liability to family and friends. I have also been able to survive because my normal response to crisis and tests of courage is to fight, rather than to freeze or flee. In such moments, I am able to call up strength and courage of which I am not aware, in my daily normal life. I will share a few examples of this.

Surviving death by a whisker and maintaining sanity comes to mind first. My utmost test of courage and fighting-back spirit came one evening in September 1996, when I was faced with two gunmen at my gate at 8.00 p.m. I had been out late doing some evaluation work in an upcountry village. It is not clear in my head where these armed men emerged from, but as the security guard opened the gate, we were shocked by a loud *bang*.

The driver froze at the steering wheel as I asked him what he had knocked. "Thieves," he muttered. I looked out my window and a man with an AK rifle was staring back. I looked at the driver's window and another man with a pistol was staring inside the car. They threw the doors open, gave us a few hard slaps in the face each, and marched us towards the house entrance.

I begged them to let the driver go, explaining to them he had nothing to do with me or them and knew nothing about my home, an appeal that fell on deaf ears. We went into the house with us walking between the two of them, after they forced me to open the door. On entering, they took the nearest first door after the corridor, which was clearly our bedroom. As we entered, I noticed with amusement that even thieves steal from one another, the lead thief quickly snatched the watch and a few necklaces by my bedside and put them in his pocket, looking behind as if to check whether his colleague thief had seen him.

They then asked us to lie down after which they tied our arms behind our backs and set about ransacking the room, packing what they thought was of value. They asked for my gold and my husband's money after they failed to find any cash. They pulled me up and asked me over and over where my husband's money was kept.

I had been praying that my husband would not come in at that moment, because I knew they had left a third man, armed, at the gate who would not hesitate to shoot him dead, like they had the guard. That period in Uganda was characterised by armed robberies involving stealing, killing, and rape. The chances of surviving one of the three was zero. I had always said to myself, if ever I am faced with a rapist during one of these episodes, I would make sure the rapist killed me.

They continued asking for my husband's money, and I kept telling them I did not know where he kept his money but finally adding on that if they did not mind, I could give them mine. For many years I wondered why I did not tell them I had his money; I suppose my feminist ideology of always wanting to be independent had not been muted. Anyway, they took the money I gave them; perhaps it was not enough, or perhaps they despised it because I told them it was my money. They still wanted my husband's money.

Suddenly, the man with a pistol pulled me close to his face and, looking intensely pointing a pistol in my ear asked me, "Do you see this gun? This is the gun that will kill you, if you do not give us your husband's money."

I knew I was about to die, but I was firm because, at the moment, I felt I was ready to die. I had used my time while lying down to flash back on my life. I asked myself one question while down: "Who would be happy to know I am dead?" Frankly, I did not come up with one single name, and I thought of my children who were now adults with a great father. I knew then that I was ready to go as a happy person leaving no debt behind. I looked back at the man holding a pistol to my ear and without fear told him, "You know what? I think today is my day to die, and I think God has sent you to kill me. You are his messenger, so if you want to kill me, go ahead, do it."

I saw the man suddenly drop his hand down from my ear. He took a look at me and then said, "Come this way," heading for the bathroom. I went in ready to fight back or die, because I was imagining *rape time has come*. He threw me face down, and I began to see hope. With my husband's tie, he tied my arms behind my back and fled.

I lay down, listening to them start our car, and when I was sure they had left, I tried to untie myself. Even as I was doing that, I wondered how such a person could have tied me with evident kindness, because it was so easy to untie myself.

It was not the same with the driver. I needed to use a knife to cut the rope they had tied his arms with. He was in such a state of shock that when I told him they had left and it was safe for him to get up so we could go out, he refused to get up. I went out alone, hoping to find the guard still alive and, if wounded, get him to hospital. They had killed him on the spot. I came back inside and was finally able to convince the driver we were safe.

A year later, when the gang was finally apprehended, I was summoned to court to identify and give evidence. Many people in my family were scared on my behalf, fearing he could come back for me, if he were not found guilty. I was so sure about what he looked like because I'd made sure to study his face, in case I had a chance to make a future reference to it in court. I had seen a birthmark on his face when he pulled me close to him, and that is what helped me to identify him. And besides, they had found our household items in his hiding place. The justice system still functioned well, and the man who had put a gun to my face got a life sentence because he had killed in other places he had robbed.

What was my silver lining in this? The fact that I was alive and not even a rape victim!! My teammates with whom I had been working offered me time off and counselling.

"Why?" I asked them. "I am alive and the best way to value this experience is to rejoice in my life spared and my work."

Resilience and the ability to move and face my challenges are characteristics I believe I inherited from my mother and her mother. They have been my shield and support in maintaining sanity. I took up swimming on my sixtieth birthday, for example, because I wanted to overcome my fear of water. I am still afraid of water, but not like before, when the fear curtailed my enjoyment of boat rides, for example.

I faced possible death of a child in 1978, when I had to drive for miles to a Mulago hospital with my daughter in a spasm from malaria, believing she would be dead by the time I arrived. I still had the presence of mind to keep my index finger between her teeth, so she did not bite off her tongue. This was a trick I had learned from my neighbour, who was a professional nurse. I was lucky she survived, because in those days it was still possible; when you turned up at an emergency you got emergency treatment. Compare that with 2016, when I turned up at a hospital emergency with my husband on a Sunday evening to be told he could not be admitted because they were too busy. Two days later, he was gone.

In 1987, he survived death when he was picked up by security operatives, simply because he looked like people the new 'liberation' regime of 1986 called "Amin's people," since he was from the West Nile. But I fearlessly went from office to office looking for anyone who could trace where he had been taken. It was somebody from the intelligence service who told me he thought he could find him, and two days later, he was brought home without the shoes, watch, jacket, or tie with which he had gone out of the house, and he was starving. Courage to fight back and confront those officials came from the certainty that my husband would not abscond from his home voluntarily. My silver moment? He was back and alive and, save for the hunger, in good health.

I never lose the opportunity to look for a silver lining when courage and resilience are tested to the limit again and again. Today, I look at the years 2014, 2015, and 2016 as my ultimate tests of courage so far. I equate that period with that of Job in the Old Testament of the Bible. Those three years were sent to test my resilience and capacity for sanity.

When my sister Emily fell sick and was diagnosed with cancer in 2015, in my mind I gave us five more years to live and love each other. But in twelve months, she was gone. I loved her so much, and I know she loved me well. We used to call each other Fifty Percent. Whenever we had a family problem that needed to be solved by money, we would call each other and say, "If you have fifty percent, we can solve the problem." This is how we were able to support our parents, some siblings, and the children of one of our brothers, who were orphaned at an early age. I felt robbed when she died, but I knew I would have to lift myself up and carry on seeing these children become independent. Today I call some of them my fifty percent, and my silver lining lies in the knowledge that together we kept our brother's children cared for until they were independent thriving adults.

Then came 2015, when my mother, who was my teacher and role model, passed away. And although I was able to see her two days before she passed away and I knew she would not survive, it was still a great shock. But she had been a great mother and teacher, and I am still able to hang on to these great moments for the silver lining.

Then 2016, when unexpected death came to my house at a time when I was still asking why my sister had gone just like that, and I felt it was simply too much. I know there is no expected death. But this was one big unexpected death.

My husband was a strong and active person. In the forty-six years we had been together, we had never either of us been in hospital for illnesses. We had just returned from Seoul, South Korea on a two-week Rotary conference, where we had had so much fun. As Rotarians we travelled around the globe together.

He felt unwell on Sunday evening, so I took him to the hospital. We were sent back home, to return on Monday morning. Less than twenty-four hours later, on Tuesday morning at 6 o'clock, when I was summoned to the Acute Care Unit, I knew he was gone. No doctor calls a non-professional to the Acute Care Unit at dawn except to break the news of the dying of their patient.

I told my niece who had stayed with me in hospital that we needed courage to walk to the Acute Care Unit, the longest walk I can remember ever taking. My husband spent his lifetime making sure the children and I were loved, well taken care of, and supported no matter what. He spent his retirement supporting me and our extended family so that I could serve my mission well. He had no ego or resentment that I was working and had a public life while he was spending time managing family in the so-called private arena.

How does one see a silver lining in this, when you lose your pillar of support? Where is the silver lining? My husband hated protracted illness and the idea of lying in bed as a dependent, with people coming in to view him (as he called it) and everybody telling him what to do. I still believe that this was his prayer being answered. I hang on that, and onto the fact that he was a good man who went without a debt to me or his children, extended family, or the world in general. A friend of mine once described him as someone you could leave your suitcase with at a bus station and come back to find him where you left, still with the suitcase. He was a good man. You have to look for your silver lining in all tribulations; without it, I would have lived without hope or thanksgiving.

People matter, no matter who you or they are.

What maintains my balance and sanity is the big lesson and understanding I learned from my mother Justina: people matter, no matter who they are or who you are. The payback is that people treat you the way you treat them. Giving people dignity reduces stress.

Once I told her I was tired of supporting one of my cousins whose bad behaviour never changed. I thought she would agree with me, because she was the one who had asked me to take on this young man. Her response was,

"When you decide to help and support a person, you must take it to its conclusion."

When I look back, I think I learnt from my mother at a young age that, because people matter, treating them well and being honest with them is a duty. My mother never minced her words, if she thought you needed to know the truth or to be told off. But she always said it with grace. I saw her arbitrating between people or sometimes dealing with people who had wronged her, but everybody would be laughing with her throughout. My mother loved and welcomed people no matter who, when, or where.

One incident that took place at home when we were young reminds me of how she always made it clear to us that we must understand that people, whoever they are, must be welcomed and treated with dignity. When we were growing up, my parents' home was a converging centre for many churchgoers on Sundays. Church leaders were always welcome. Every Sunday and Christmas, we prepared food for a feast of many, even when no one we knew was invited.

There was one particular Sunday when time for serving lunch came and there were no visitors. As children, we were happy, because this time we were each going to have a proper piece of chicken. As we sat down with a piece on each of our plates, my mother came to the dining room with urgency, asking who still had a piece of chicken intact.

I was always the slowest eater, in spite of boarding school life. My piece of chicken was visible and intact. Gracefully, my mother picked it and put it on a clean plate, explaining she had seen a person at some distance and was sure this person was coming to our home, guessing they would be our visitor for lunch. She reminded us of the shame she would experience if a guest watched us, her children, enjoying a piece of chicken. It was more important for the guest to know he was expected. The message was that he was an expected guest and his portion had been set aside, waiting his arrival. I learned how to give dignity to a human being.

Building networks and strong support systems reduces stress

Years later, I came to appreciate that my mother's way was an important process for creating supportive networks. When all the children of my parents were educated and left home and migrated to the city, the only people my aged parents had left nearby who really cared for them were the local community members: churchgoers who came for lunch on Sundays; women she taught health and nutrition to; and families she had reconciled. I often think of them and how they supported my parents; I also cringe in shame that at some point of my life I felt unhappy because I had lost a piece of chicken to one of them.

My lesson from this is, when you forget humanity, you cannot create networks of support; and when you do not have support, sometimes you lose sanity. I learned the importance of this when I was doing my graduate studies in Minnesota University, where I had gone with my children, leaving their father (my husband) behind for the first time in our partnership. I was able to quickly create a network of friends who would come in to take care of the children and take us shopping. It was possible to maintain my sanity because of the strong networks of support I built. I also learned that to create them you must first build trust.

My friends and family know they can count on me. When I promise I will deliver, I make sure that I do, and it will be quality. This is also possible when you know your limitations.

Non-Negotiable Values

These are core values upon which I have based my life. These values are those things on which you would not be willing to compromise, even if it were popular, profitable, or justifiable to do so. (M. McQueen)

What are my non-negotiables?

1. Balancing expectations is a non-negotiable

I learnt to say no, if I knew I could not deliver, rather than make false promises. All the people I have worked with know, if I am unable to deliver on something, I will tell them there and then. A friend of mine once told a group of people, when introducing me, "With Dr. Tadria, what you see is what you get."

I found this also helps me to achieve balance by making sure I do not make false promises. That way, no one will pursue me to the point of upsetting my mental health because I failed to deliver. In Uganda, most people say, "I will see what I can do." My response is that this is a clear sign that they already know they will not carry through for you.

I have learnt that balancing expectations starts with understanding one's capabilities and the system in which one operates. When you create false expectations, you attract demands you cannot meet. The social system most of us operate in, especially Uganda, has created a normative framework that puts undue expectations on women. We are told we are the mothers of the nation and a mother cannot go wrong; we are the cooks and the only caregivers. When we try to meet all these expectations, however, we become submissive to the point of self-abuse, but we are told it is okay because we are women. As women, we have fallen into this trap of expectations. Even as a woman, I learned to say no to the cultural expectations of patriarchy.

2. Daring to be different

Daring to be different is another non-negotiable. I have a right to be different: I have dealt with the unrealistic expectations and balanced my different identities by daring to be different. I have had a gift of both informal and formal education that has enabled me to understand how this system of patriarchy works. I have had the courage to make a decision that, if the norm does not work for me, I will work outside the norm. This has given me the ability to say no to prescribed expectations. This is the message I carry with me when I train young people, both girls and boys: you can say no to the social prescriptions that do not work for you. You must dare to stand up and be different.

The nurturing I received in my family (informal education) taught me that these expectations are negotiable, because I saw my mother living outside the norm and negotiating for her right to participate, lead, and be happy. The image I have of my mother is of a joyful person but also an assertive woman. The kind of person antifeminists would classify as a stubborn woman. It is this character and agency that enabled her to engage in public life, joining party politics at a time when it was almost taboo for women. She was also an entrepreneur, personally managing a public transport business.

My mother spoke out in public with a clear, loud voice without self-censorship and was always invited on committees, both at local and national level. She was not afraid to propose alternative ways of doing things to my father; and I never heard my father silence her because she was a woman and his wife.

As children, my parents encouraged healthy debates among us all, without silencing the girls. There were no specific roles of girls and boys in my parents' home; we all cooked, washed dishes, and fetched water together. But in addition, the roles of boys were to fetch firewood and tend the goats; but they are also roles my younger sisters were called upon to perform later, as the boys, who were older in our pack of eleven siblings, transitioned from home to boarding schools. My father understood very well that my mother was different and never demanded his food be prepared only by his wife; in reality, my mother only supervised, even when she was around. I learned early on that the roles of women/girls and men/boys could be fluid, and all could perform them well. I have a brother who boasted of being the best at making millet bread, a strictly female-classified role.

I went through same-sex boarding schools none the wiser. Until I got to university, where my willingness to answer questions loud and clear, and my rejection of being taken out by boys when I had my own money became topics of conversation—and not flattering ones for that matter. Later on in life, I learnt from friends that during my university years I was classified as too arrogant and intelligent to be taken out by men; but it is really because I dared to be different. I loved my life, though, because I had a goal and being different protected me, so I was not vulnerable to sexual harassment.

My formal education, especially, began to fine-tune my home informal education when I took a course in women's studies in my doctoral program. I started to understand how this system has perfected the allocation of powers and privileges for one sex (mainly male), with the support of another sex (mainly female). I understood how public and private space structural arrangements are put in place to sustain the powers and privileges of one group/sex and discriminate against the other. I was able to understand my mother's frustrations and the criticisms she received from the community for her public-life engagement and speaking out; it was a result of her breaking the barriers of patriarchal normative structures and rules. I also understood the basis of the discriminations and antagonisms from male colleagues I had experienced at different stages of my life.

Well-armed with my mother's life experiences and the empowering upbringing I received, together with a clear theoretical understanding of how and why the patriarchal system works, I was fully prepared for the act of balancing my life. My role was to make it clear to all concerned that I dared to be different because I had a right to be; to stand in the public space, to speak out, and to say no, if I needed to.

When my boyfriend, a Ugandan gentleman I had met at Cambridge University who later became my husband, suggested that he would like to marry me, my immediate reaction was to stand up for my right and dignity by letting him know I would not be a "normal housewife." My response was that I would like us like to be married, but I also let him know I would not iron shirts or get up in the middle of the night to serve him dinner, just because we were married.

I then set out to make a list of the things I would not do and the things I love to do and would be willing to continue doing; this included the red lights he would not be allowed to cross. I had heard stories of my female compatriots being beaten or left by their husbands for not living within the prescribed norms of the "system" of patriarchy. I was setting my boundaries of expectations, outside the patriarchal normative framework. It was then that my husband told me he had learned to cook in his home and nothing was going to change. He knew how to wash and clean because he, too, was from a family where many of the elder siblings were boys, so he knew how to look after children. I knew then that we would be equal partners, supporting each other because he accepted my difference.

Throughout our married life of forty-six years, he proved to be the greatest support in making sure I was able to balance my international professional and feminist work with my personal life and to maintain my sanity.

Most times, girls and women do not know there is an alternative way of living and that they can live it, if they dare to be different. Sometimes, punishment for breaking the patriarchal norms can be brutal if you are not well prepared for it. I tell young people my story about how I negotiated my marriage as a learning point around how you can design your relationships; but not if your requirements are debatable or relationships are transactional.

Working with young women, one gets to understand why it is usually difficult for them to balance life and usually opt out of work outside the home. I have learned and come to appreciate that not many girls have had the benefit of being nurtured in an environment that has trained or taught them that there is an alternative life to the prescribed cultural norms which are many times working against their interest. Because they do not know the possibility exists, oftentimes young women (and men) enter into partnerships where they have not clarified the non-negotiables, i.e., the red lines not to be crossed. The truth of the matter is if, as a man, you have power and privilege, you may not be willing to lose them; but must you exercise them at the expense of the women in your life?

What my learning has taught me and what I try to pass on is this: do not settle for less, do not set boundaries that limit your space, and do not accept imposed normative cultural standards that you know you cannot meet. Most important, speak out and learn to say no. Even in a society like Uganda, where young people are being taught to think that marriage is the ultimate prize, people need to learn that marriage can be a poisoned chalice, if one goes into it as an unequal partner, without rights, voice, or agency. In a relationship where there is a privilege/power and a subservient binary, inequality is inevitable; that is what will create imbalance and violence at one point or another, likely sooner rather than later.

3. **Defining and maintaining clarity and focusing on my priorities is another non-negotiable**

Once you set your priorities, you stop sweating the small stuff and start to balance your work and personal life.

The trivial things I refused to fuss about, for example, were the negative things that people said about me working outside my country without my husband, i.e., abandoning him; and how they were reacting to the fact that I was now getting higher income than him. Many people had "issues" with us putting our children in boarding schools, forgetting that these children were among the few going to particularly good schools at the time. This was an opportunity and privilege that shaped their lives and those of their children.

When my husband and I agreed to go into a marriage partnership, our goal was to have a focus on family health, stability, a good standard of living and respect for each other, and well-educated children who would be able to know and enjoy living in different worlds beyond the prescribed boundaries. These were the agreed-upon priorities and goals of our family. These are the core values we both committed to bring/contribute to our family.

My family was a partnership between my husband and me, as well as our children and other interested parties, especially our parents and siblings. This is why together we could defy the normative standards of patriarchy. We were very clear about what our family was going to look like as well as our goals in life, and because of that there was no conflict between my personal life and my commitment to professionalism. They were both centred on a shared vision of the kind of life my husband and I wanted for ourselves and our children.

Does it mean we did not have challenges? No, it does not. But, as a family, we were happy because we were focused on the vision of what we wanted for our family, and it was centred in the core values we had defined for ourselves: trust, respect, dependability, and dignity. At no time would one treat the other as less than themselves.

One of the agreements we made when getting married was that marriage would not get in the way of the other's professional life; also, that we would do what was needed to support professional achievement and excellency when called upon. That is why, during the most difficult time of Uganda in early eighties, my husband was happy to stay behind in Uganda while I went to the United States of America with "his children" (as some people said) to do my doctorate, when he himself did not have one. Most of our friends and colleagues never understood the reasons for our choices. My own employers in Makerere University, including my immediate manager, tried to discourage me from going—"in the interest of my husband," they said. But as a family we understood I could not progress as a lecturer in the University without a higher education, and that an opportunity of travel for our children to another country and culture could not be harmful. On the contrary, we would not be able to forgive ourselves if we fell below the standards of professionalism we had set or shirked the ability to deliver a quality life to ourselves.

4. **Walking the talk as a feminist and building an organisation that works for the women and men who work for it: this was an important non-negotiable feminist value for me.**

Value 1: I set up MEMPROW with a feminist mind-set and determined that it must work for those who worked for it. The evidence for this is that the organisation has exceptionally low staff turnover. In its twelve years of existence, only two staff members left by choice. One left, and in her admission, it was because she was afraid of how MEMPROW would work after leadership change. Another one left because she felt she had been mentored well enough to start another, MEMPROW-like initiative.

Value 2: Respecting my body with what I feed it, emotionally and physically, is important for my feminist journey and work. My team always wants to know what I eat that keeps me alert, no matter what time of the day. Healthy eating is one of my core health value that I brought into the work space where I know it appreciated. Feeding my brain with up-to-date information is also a core value I brought into the organisation which is now known and appreciated as a learning organisation.

Value 3: When I established the organisation, I wanted to build an entity where power of all sorts (power in knowledge, visibility, skills, and leadership) would be shared. Capacity building is an imperative in feminist leadership. If the leader is the only holder of knowledge, the organisation is bound to fail. At MEMPROW, we have invested in staff learning, as well as in staff wellbeing. We have been deliberate in expanding their local and international spaces and perspectives. There is no professional staff member who has not travelled out of Uganda to engage in regional or global discourse. Together, we have strived to build a feminist organisation with a "soul," where everybody is somebody with voice and agency, and where we know, if one person fails, we have all failed. First, we have failed her, and then we have failed the organisation.

Value 4: Delivering on our core work professionally. As a feminist, I was not prepared to compromise on mentoring a team of young women and building a professional organisation that worked for quality results and strong positive stewardship for resources entrusted to us in the name of women and girls. The evidence that MEMPROW staff and I have consistently walked the feminist talk is in staff testimonies. These also show their preparedness to take on the mantle and sustain girls' mentoring and women's leadership from a feminist and human rights perspective. This is mainly because they have been mentored well to be professional, to be good stewards, and to have a soul; in short, to be feminists.

In this section, I share their testimonies as validation of the power of mentoring and in building an organisation with a soul, one that works for the people who work for it.

My MEMPROW Story: Sarah Nakame: Programmes Director

My name is Sarah Nakame, and this is my story. Growing up, I was fascinated by my mom and how, without a senior 4 certificate, she ably gathered women in our home to do life together. She was so active in different spaces, including local council meetings where she was given leadership, and mother union in the different Anglican churches we attended. You see, she barely knew much English, but her confidence and leadership stood out when she talked about women's leadership and strength in numbers. I knew I would in one way or the other follow in her footsteps. When I joined the Mentoring and Empowerment Programme for Young Women, I knew this was it and that a great door had opened for me.

I joined MEMPROW shortly after university. As a fresh university graduate, I was proud of my shorthand and colloquial language — it stood out in how I spoke and wrote. Meeting Dr. Tadria, I quickly learned that something had to be done with my language, and yes, I spoke English, Uganda's national formal language.

Learning professional writing and communication skills was one of my first transformations under the mentorship of Dr. Tadria. You see, when you have graduated from the best university, it's believable that you would have good command of English language and be able to differentiate between formal and informal communication; unfortunately, that was not the case for me.

Being the person of high standards Dr. Tadria is, it was known that she would not put her signature on a letter or document whose content was not thoroughly done. Oh, how I wrote and rewrote even thirty-word emails before clicking send. In fact, in order to ensure quality, we never sent emails before inviting at least two colleagues to read and confirm it was good. Looking back, I am proud of my writing skills and thankful that Dr. Tadria did not compromise on quality, regardless of how painful it might have felt to write and rewrite the same document until it was signature-worthy.

Flights, national and international work engagements

Growing up, my sisters and brothers and many children in my play group and neighbourhood enjoyed waving at aeroplanes that passed over our compounds. It was a fascinating reverie. I don't remember ever having given too much thought to flying, apart from knowing it was a means of transport for people to move from one continent to another. For me, it was not an achievement I prioritised— after all, I did not know many close relatives who flew or whose work crossed border.

Shortly after joining MEMPROW, I had a bewildering experience: my first flight! Who forgets their first flight? In fact, it was so good that I celebrated my birthday in 2009 by the Atlantic Ocean, at a hotel beach in Liberia. That, too, was my introduction to international practice and an invitation to the world of global feminist movement-building. It was also my first experience having a large sum of money that was given as DSA. The excitement for me and my family is unforgettable, and just like that I became their global citizen.

I am thankful that MEMPROW opened doors for me to the experiences of women across nations, which helped me know that our problems may be different but are also similar in many ways. International experience enabled me understand the systemic and complex connections between the issues, politics, and challenges of the fight for equity and equality for women.

It's easy to think one knows a great deal about their country, if they took history, geography, and social studies at school. Realistically, that's not the case. MEMPROW works in communities in the West Nile region and the Eastern region. This means I got to travel a lot in those areas. I cannot say enough how much this opened me up to appreciating our "Ugandaness," as opposed to which tribe, which region one comes from.

I must also say that my experiences in these rural communities shaped my political orientation, putting me face to face with girls with shattered dreams after parents forced them into marriage; pupils studying under trees or schools with girls but without a single female teacher;

communities with barely enough food for their children; and teenage mothers. I could go on and on. These opportunities to work with such communities made me believe that change is possible and that our MEMPROW programmes change lives.

On Professionalism

Working at MEMPROW has shaped my professional life in many ways. My undergraduate study was in adult and community education; it prepared me for the workplace. MEMPROW sharpened the language skills required for the workplace; professional etiquette and time-keeping are also things I have directly learned under Dr. Tadria's mentorship.

When Dr. Tadria gives her word, she keeps it; she also models good stewardship of resources, accountability, and deliverance on work within planned time frames. For the entire time I worked with Dr. Tadria and MEMPROW, when we committed to a project/programme or cause, it was done, unless circumstances were completely outside of our control. Her professional approach to building and maintaining relationships is something that stands out, because of which MEMPROW's resource base grew to where it is now. I am truly thankful that I have had the opportunity to be mentored and shaped by Dr. Tadria.

People often say, "Do as I say but not as I do," but the reverse is true with Dr. Tadria. I have had a secret admiration for how she carries herself, and how she keeps her body and mind alert at all times. Sometimes I would get angry at myself when I could not remember details of something, and yet she can recount every story of the girls or community members we interfaced with during any of our activities, word for word. Then I learned to be keen, to be present.

I have been at MEMPROW for a long time. I have done or been part of most programmes, including intergenerational mentoring and gender dialogues, the MEMPROW Girls Network, social survival skills trainings, girls' newsletter, and most other organisation documents and reports. I am sure Dr. Tadria will know all the dates, because I have not found a person with a brain as alert as hers. I still wonder why God did not gift me abundantly with this ability. She taught me the importance of listening actively and being interested in our stakeholders. I journey on for this desired ability with persistence.

In short, my body, mind, and soul have been nurtured and groomed by Dr. Tadria. I am eternally grateful for her leadership. I cannot not say it has all been rosy. Of course, I have had personal challenges and tests with the team along the way. What I am sure kept me with my head above the water and focused on MEMPROW's vision, however, was Dr. Tadria's leadership. She ensures that she handles all team members individually and not as one big unit. She steadily nudges one to excellence with calmness and reassurance, so at MEMPROW, I knew it was okay to make mistakes as long as you learn from them.

I am thankful to Dr. Tadria and MEMPROW for giving me the opportunity to grow my wings.

చిచిచిచి

My MEMPROW Story: Fred Kigozi: Finance and Administration Officer

Mid-2008, I met Dr. Hilda Tadria. She had just founded an organisation, a company limited by guarantee. Its name was Mentoring and Empowerment Programme for Women (MEMPROW). I had been recommended to her to help in the areas of financial record-keeping for the organisation. At the time, I had little or no experience of working for non-governmental or charity organisations, which was the major business for MEMPROW, but I gradually improved with time under her guidance.

For a while, I worked on a part-time basis but soon got on the payroll on a contract basis. Little did I know I would spend the next twelve years working alongside her, under her guidance. But this has not come as a surprise, since I had worked in several different places but had never had a chance to work with a women's rights activist. At first, I thought that, being a man, I wouldn't fit into the organisation, but I quickly found out this was not the case. Dr. Tadria exhibited a high standard of work ethics. She was very dedicated to her job as the Executive Director, always making sure that the organisation was run on solid human rights, no matter the gender.

I soon realised MEMPROW was a second home to me. The environment at work was too homey. I remember one time when I was living alone with my sons (their mother was travelling); they were quite young and the responsibilities were overwhelming. Dr. Tadria realised this and called me to her office. I think she saw the stress I was under. She asked me what was wrong, and I explained. She advised that I work half-day for some time, until I got my home life sorted out. I had never experienced this throughout my working life in any other place. I was touched by her thoughtfulness and insight.

Another incident was work-related. I had messed up on something, and while we were discussing it, something within me snapped and I lost it... I lost my mind, shouted back at her, and moved out of her office. Within seconds of sitting at my desk, I realised I had made one of the biggest mistakes of my life. I knew this was the end; I had lost my job. I looked into my drawers to see if there were any personal items of mine, for I thought, the moment she came out of her office, she was going to hand me a termination letter.

I was wrong. Instead, she came out and asked me to follow her to the office gardens for a talk. I could not believe it. We talked about the issue that was at hand, and I remember how my eyes teared a lot. I left the gardens wondering what kind of person she was. That night, when I was at home, I thought it through. I thought about the many incidents that had happened between her and other staff and the way she had handled them. It dawned on me, to me, Dr. Tadria was not only a women's rights activist or the Executive Director of MEMPROW, as I had known her; she possessed other virtues not common with most people. The one thing I cannot forget about her is her compassion and empathy. To me, Dr. Tadria is like a mother and a mentor.

Thank you, Dr. Tadria. You have made, mentored and moulded me into what I am today.

જ

My MEMPROW Story : Lilian Nalwoga: Programmes Manager

Working with this reputable organization that has invested in my growth gives me a feeling of self-appreciation. MEMPROW has a learning culture that has developed my knowledge and competence. It has unlocked opportunities for personal transformation and has continuously developed my sense of responsibility and accountability, an identity not just for me but every colleague with whom we serve in this organization.

On numerous occasions, people are motivated by the monetary considerations that accrue from their professional engagements but tend to ignore the most fundamental impacts such engagements have on their lives, like the valuable experience and adventurous human interaction. In this amazing journey, I have encountered remarkably amazing women. I am talking about women who matter. I have had the pleasure to share some of their success stories. These self-driven women have numerous inspirational stories about work and life.

I have on various quarterly evaluations quoted Dr. Tadria, asking, "Do you wake up in the morning and still feel like you should be at MEMPROW?" Without hesitation my answer is usually *YES*, a genuine response and not one tainted by bias; a reflection of what I truly feel. Working here is always exciting and offers something new to learn on a daily basis.

My interaction with MEMPROW was quite timely. It was an opportunity that presented itself when it was most needed. I recall my first interaction with Dr. Tadria. She was an elegant and engaging woman. In fact, I remember during the job interview, when she asked me whether I was married, I was quick to say yes. Naïve as I was at that time, marriage meant having cohabited with a man for years. I remember her telling me, "Lillian, you are not married."

As a feminist with comprehensive knowledge about gender and the patriarchy that still pervades this world, she quickly foresaw the fate that awaited a mother of three who had innocently engaged herself in a cohabitation she had mistaken for a marriage, with no sound legal basis. However, this is not to say that marriage is a great achievement to any woman, but at this particular point in time, it pointed to stability, and I had to sort out this specific part of my life. This was a time of enlightenment, and with her mentoring, I started getting out of my comfort zone to understand my hidden fears that could sabotage me at any given time. This necessitated the use of feminist lenses to start seeing things differently. The rest is history.

I have always been astounded by the support at MEMPROW. It is a great pleasure working under a leadership that sees the potential in you that others, including yourself, might not see; a leadership that gives you the courage to find your own path in the best way. Through mentorship, a lot is now possible. It has enabled me to explore heights I had never dreamt of.

One other memorable scenario was during my early days at MEMPROW, when we had to present a paper on girls' performance and retention in education in Zambia. Sarah, my partner, and I did the research and prepared the presentation for Dr. Tadria; she was to do the final presentation, as she was the expert, or so we thought. To my surprise, Dr. Tadria told me to present it.

"I can't," I said.

"Of course, you can," she responded encouragingly, and indeed I did execute it. This taught me never to turn down an opportunity; to always try or at least learn on the job, but to never say "I can't." I have learnt to pursue my goals with passion, to always question the story behind each conclusion, and to see the potential in every human being, because as staff we are endowed differently but accepted the same. The mentoring has given me confidence and self-belief that have enabled me to defy incredible odds.

Another important aspect has been my family relationships, specifically that with my children and parenting. Raising children is one of the toughest yet still most fulfilling endeavours, and often the one we feel least prepared for. I laud MEMPROW for having improved my parenting skills.

Working with girls from different communities with various family backgrounds has equipped me with more effective approaches for raising my children. In the long run, I have become a mother to all. I have become more meticulous and compassionate, and the improved interaction skills have enabled me to be a better parent. This has given me a deeper understanding of my children; I have been able to improve their confidence and communication skills. This opportunity provided by MEMPROW has given me satisfaction insofar as I have been able to equip my children with basic skills I lacked as a child.

I know it took me many years to even realise how thoroughly I had been indoctrinated by the messages I received from society that affected my self-esteem. However, in the long run I have been able to inspire many girls and young women. My hope is always that girls can be empowered, with their voices heard in a relatively timely manner, and that it does not take them as much time as it took me. Girls need to be helped to find their sense of self and sense of purpose, to learn that their voices matter, to embrace their uniqueness and true identity, and to believe in their dreams.

Working with MEMPROW has helped me to slowly gain insight into my own voice and power. I can comfortably say I have gained my "aha" moment. I am ready to continue lighting the candle with genuineness and honesty. Thank you, MEMPROW, for allowing me to escape my shell.

ക്ക്ക്ക്

My MEMPROW Story: Immaculate Mukasa: Current Executive Director

When I joined MEMPROW in 2015 as a Senior Programme Manager, I knew there was a lot to learn from the female-led organisation. Three months into work, some things were not progressing as smoothly as I had expected. After a long time of contemplation, I posed this question to Dr. Hilda Mary Tadria, my supervisor, who is also the Executive Director: "Why is it that when I request feedback from some staff, their response is not positive and the facial expression communicates 'a bother'?"

Her response was unexpected, deep, and it reaffirmed my role and calling. She said, "If it was a male requesting the feedback, they would positively respond and possibly say that he was good at his work." That statement formed one of my hinges for courage to face barriers and overcome them.

I knew it was not about me or my colleagues at work, but patriarchal systems and structures that sometimes infiltrate attitudes and unconsciously inform our responses. We therefore have to be deliberate in the struggle against patriarchy. It is noticeably clear that Dr. Tadria is a leader with genuine expertise, high competence, and knowledge in gender and leadership. Indeed, from the time we first met, by observing and listening to her, I have learnt and appreciated her competence, championship, character, and charisma.

Dr. Tadria's diligence and vigilance are unquestionable. Sometimes, work is too hectic, but Dr. Tadria continuously demonstrates perseverance and determination to perform tasks. "As long as I am required to participate, let me know and I will be there." This is always her statement of assurance, as we plan for activities to be executed. Even now, she willingly travels by road to the West Nile region of Uganda, about 470 kilometres, to reach communities in

Zombo, Arua, Nebbi, and Pakwach. She is personally a strong producer, who gets good results consistently and exercises good judgement.

Within MEMPROW, she has inspired and motivated us to act for personal and professional advancement. In addition, she taught us to discover the unique talents and personalities that each staff member brings to the organisation. She reinforces and strengthens the positives in people while keeping a lid on their negatives. As a result, MEMPROW builds on the uniqueness of its staff for increased productivity, and every member is and feels valued.

She connects with everyone in a unique way. She works across boundaries and builds collaborative relationships. This is reflected in the number and diversity of stakeholders she rallies to support girls and women, ranging from individuals, families, and institutions to the formation of chapters of MEMPROW in Zimbabwe, Zambia, Botswana, and South Africa. Dr. Tadria is a matchless, seasoned leader who has steered MEMPROW with innovative ideas, strategic thinking, and tireless efforts to increase its visibility and credibility. We are blessed that we will continue learning from her as a Board member.

It's impossible to write down all ways MEMPROW has mentored me. I joined MEMPROW in February 2015. Time has passed and lessons have been learnt. When I first signed onto the MEMPROW team, I was naïve with little knowledge about women's rights and leadership. I wasn't critical about the challenges affecting girls and women, because society had normalised them. In addition, I was insensitive; I contributed to stereotyping other women and girls. I was timid, and I could not speak in public.

At MEMPROW, I have received a vast body of knowledge ranging from human rights, gender and patriarchy, feminism, leadership, etc. I found a safe space; a space that nurtured me to be strong, courageous, and confident, to know my rights and to negotiate in relationships. I have learnt, unlearnt, and relearnt.

The seeds that have been planted bear fruit daily. I am a champion in advocating for the safety of women and their rights; my passion for working with women has grown. I became intentional in supporting my fellow women. For instance, when I go to the market, my first priority is to buy from a woman. This stems from the realisation that most of these women have been abandoned and are the sole providers for their children at home. In my circles, I tell my friends whenever I sense violence against human/women's rights. I have made my stand clear: zero tolerance to violence. Even my male friends know I have no sympathy in the event they abuse women.

MEMPROW taught me that women, too, need financial independence. I have pushed my siblings and friends to break those boundaries that have been socially constructed to limit us as women. One testimony I have is that of a friend whose husband refused to allow her to continue with university. She had stayed home for more than eight years. We had conversations until she was courageous enough to face her husband, and she is currently completing her bachelor's degree.

I cannot talk about my journey without mentioning how professional MEMPROW is. I must say that these five years have been significant in my career. I have put organisational values coupled with mine at the forefront of what I do. Every day when I wake up, I think of how to do things in line with my feminist principles.

Thanks to the team, with special thanks to Dr. Tadria, who took me under her wing; her leadership and example have helped me to grow my potential, I found my purpose. She is an inspiration and fantastic at her job. I salute her tenacity of purpose and outstanding leadership qualities, especially her level of integrity, which is unmatched. She has relentlessly mentored me; she inspired me to grow beyond my limits in my career, academics, and personal life. I cannot forget her motherly tender heart that allowed me to bring my whole self to work and the warmth that comes with her smile—it brightens so many of my days. Thank you for being a pillar of strength. Long live you and your MEMPROW Legacy!

༚ཚྭཚྭཚྭཚྭ

MY JOURNEY AT MEMPROW: Doris Nalwanga

It's impossible to write all ways MEMPROW has mentored me. I joined MEMPROW in February 2015, time has passed and lessons have been learnt. When I first signed on the MEMPROW team, I was naïve with little knowledge about women rights and leadership. I wasn't critical about the challenges affecting girls and women because society had normalized them. In addition I was insensitive; I contributed to stereotyping other women and girls. I was timid and I could not speak in public.

At MEMPROW, I have received a vast of knowledge raging from human rights, gender and patriarchy, feminism, leadership etc. I found a safe space; a space that nurtured me to be strong, courageous and confident, know my rights and negotiate in relationships. I have Learnt, unlearnt, and relearnt.

The seed that have been planted bears fruit daily; I am champion in advocating for safety of women and their rights; my passion for working with women has grown. I became intentional in supporting my fellow women for instance when I go to the market, my first priority is a women. This stems from the realization that most of these women have been abandoned and are the sole providers of their children/at homes. In my circles, I tell my friends when I sense violence of human/women's rights. I have made my stand clear; zero tolerance to violence even my male friends know I have no solace in the event they abuse women.

MEMPROW taught me that women, too, need financial independence; I have pushed my siblings, friends to break those boundaries socially constructed to limit us as women. One testimony is of a friend whose husband had refused her to continue with university, she had stayed home for more than eight years; we had conversations until she was courageous to face her husband. She is currently completing her bachelor's degree.

I cannot talk about my journey without mentioning how professional MEMPROW is. I must say that these five years have been significant in my career; I have put organizational values coupled with mine at the forefront of what I do. Every day when I wake up, I am thinking of how to do things right in line with my feminist principles.

Thanks to the team, special thanks to Dr. Tadria who took me under her wings; her leadership and example has helped me to grow my potential, I found my purpose. She is an inspiration and fantastic at her job, I salute her tenacity of purpose and outstanding leadership qualities especially her level of integrity that is unmatched. She has relentless mentored me; she inspired me to grow beyond my limits in my career, academics and personal life. I cannot forget her motherly tender heart that allows me to bring my whole self to work and the warmth that comes with her smile brightens so many of my days. Thank you for being a pillar of strength. Long live your and MEMPROW Legacy!

∝∽∝∽

My MEMPROW Story: Mercy Grace Munduru: Programme Manager

MEMPROW's uniqueness lies in the feminist foundation established by Dr. Tadria, the networks far and wide that the organisation is a part of, and in acknowledging our niche while continuing to focus our growth to better what we are already good at. Dr. Tadria has taught us what Og Mandino referred to in his book, *The Greatest Miracle in the World,* as "rag-pickers," which ordinarily refers to the act of identifying individuals who have lost their sense of self-worth and self-esteem, then rebuilding them and boosting their confidence in their own abilities. In the feminist context, Dr. Tadria has practiced the art of "caring for one another," and it has worked perfectly well, an act that must be acknowledged, documented, and replicated.

The values such as transparency, accountability, honesty, and teamwork are deeply entrenched in every member of staff. This was one of the most amazing qualities I admired about MEMPROW when I just joined. It feels safe to grow in a well-cultivated workspace. I personally continue to grow and learn from those who came before me. MEMPROW was a worthwhile venture in my career path.

ঔঔঔঔ

My MEMPROW Story: Stella Oyungrwoth Programme Officer

Working as a social worker was something I never thought of doing. All my life I dreamt of working in a financial institution, which never happened, even after studying accounting and finance at the University.

I joined MEMPROW exactly two years and two months ago and have been working as a project officer, field based. I still remember the question Dr. Hilda Tadria asked me during my first phone conversation with her: "Is this the kind of job you want to do?" I smiled and said yes, even before knowing what it would be like practically. But today I will add, I *love* what I am doing. That is why I always give it my all.

Although I did not have much experience working directly with communities, MEMPROW's mentorship made it possible and amazingly simple. I still remember how I feared but also admired Dr. Tadria and the rest of the team for the tough job they had been doing for the young generation of girls.

I earlier said this job was made simple by the team, but I also want to thank my family for supporting my growth. Many times, I got back from the field almost drained by the kind of trauma these girls had gone through at such a tender age. Yet I pushed through, because I was determined to do my job well. I still laugh at myself every time I look back on my fear when I joined, wondering how I would be able to pull through with Dr. Tadria, who seemed very straight with everyone. But I sat back and asked myself why I should be worried, as long as I could do the right thing as required at the right time and deliver.

With time, I saw the character of two people who raised me up to be the person I am today in Dr. Tadria: my mother and sister. With that I knew I would pull through after all. So, working and worrying about her became much less as I did my job with her. Truth is nothing great I ever did was ever accomplished alone. For every goal I have achieved, I can trace back each one to a mentor or individuals who helped me achieve it and, in this case, to Dr. Tadria and the rest of the team at MEMPROW.

Working and mentorship at MEMPROW have helped me learn that no one is ever too big for the other, no matter the position. Many times, we shared meals, laughter, and jokes as we worked. I never at one point felt like a junior, because I was treated as any other employee working to achieve the same organizational goals. I was always given a chance and an opportunity to do something and do it excellently.

I also realised that working as a team contributed greatly to my career. Somehow, I always had another colleague readily offering support and guiding me to do things the right way, when I needed them. I have learnt quite a number of things through Dr. Tadria's mentorship, most importantly about delivering work very well and timely, plus giving others a chance to grow.

I have been able to rediscover myself and learn how to identify myself with something I love, which is working with young people and empowering them. This is because, for the past two years working with MEMPROW, when I look at the stories of change from the young girls, I feel overwhelmed that at least I was part of their journey of transformation. And because I made an impact on that person, I feel empowered.

At MEMPROW, they do not only care about your career but also your personal (physical, social, mental, and emotional) health, as all these contribute greatly to one's performance at work. This kind of looking out for one another has kept every employee fit. I admire and appreciate such kind of resilience from each one at MEMPROW.

My MEMPROW Story: Patience Kwiocwiny: Programme Officer

Working with MEMPROW was literally my first formal job after graduating with a bachelor's degree in business administration. I saw myself working in a financial institution after I graduated, though I was often advised to have an open mind when its came to job opportunities, especially in today's job market.

When I started working with MEMPROW, I was introduced and welcomed as one of the staff by all the staff members and by Dr. Tadria, who was then the Executive Director and founder of MEMPROW.

Working with MEMPROW has changed a lot of things in my life. These changes include the acquisition of knowledge, capacity building, self-esteem, exposure, and above all an attitude change. Before I joined MEMPROW, together with the other community members, I would blame a victim of rape and defilement, asking her questions like, "Where were you? What were you wearing? What time was it?" I would allocate blame and build stories around the circumstances, stories that would seek out culpability for the victim. But now, I know that both boys and girls have equal rights, including where to be at what time and how to dress. I realised that the most important thing communities need is an attitude change and access to information.

I have managed to influence and share my personal change stories with several people, starting right from home by treating everyone equally, including encouraging children to participate in decision-making. In the communities around me, I am able to look at teenage mothers differently as people who should not be blamed but helped, so they can have better futures. I now have the confidence to share with others about violence against women and girls and equal rights. I feel so happy when I cause a girl to be taken back to school, especially those from within my community. I remember encouraging my colleague, whenever we were facing challenges in the field, by asking her where girls like us would be if people like Dr. Tadria had not worked extremely hard.

In MEMPROW, with the leadership of Dr. Tadria, we are not just a family but a united family where everyone looks out for each other. Dr. Tadria's common saying that always rings in my mind is, if one of us fails, the whole organization fails. This I remember in each and everything I do, and it encourages me to work harder.

I have worked with MEMPROW for one year and ten months, and I never regret anything. I continue to pray and hope that, I can be a woman of purpose to those I get to interact with through MEMPROW.

My MEMPROW Story: Doreen Kyasiimire, Programme Manager-MEMPROW

I joined the Mentoring and Empowerment Programme for Young Women (MEMPROW) as a fresh graduate from Makerere University. I had always looked forward to working in an organisation that promotes gender equality because of my background in women and gender studies. MEMPROW has been a stepping stone in my career through the opportunities it has laid before me. Having to work with young women, positively impacting their daily lives has been very fulfilling. Dr. Hilda. M. Tadria has been acting as senior mentor not only career wise but also in a much holistic manner that has helped me go through everyday life. MEMPROW made a profound impact in my career when I was given a study leave of two years to further my education at Carlton University in Canada. My 3 year work experience at MEMPROW was a major factor of my selection as the only Ugandan student out of over 1000 applicants.

Similarly, due to the continuous mentoring from Dr. Hilda. M. Tadria, I managed to survive in a diverse, multi-cultural society and graduated with a master of Public Policy and Administration. MEMPROW'S values and principles have encouraged me to think of myself as a woman of substance, one who is able to achieve her life aspirations no matter what comes my way. The frequent interaction with young women, getting to know how much they have to endure in a system that undermines girls and women's rights has taught me to be more empathetic and committed to bringing positive change.

As the famous quote goes "Change will not come if we wait for some other person or some other time. We are the ones we have been waiting for. We are the change we want." (Barack Obama) Dr. Atria's legacy is that of leaving behind a changed society that respects, values and is safe for young women. I am proud to be among the many girls whose lives have been positively impacted, and I vow to continue being an agent of change. The change will start with me and spread to the people that I interact with in order to make a safe space for young women.

CONCLUSION

THE MEMPROW TRAIN[38]

MEMPROW, like all organisations I have started, is a child born out of my feminist rage about what is happening to girls and young women today. Most especially, it is about my rage around a culture of silence that shrouds defilement and domestic violence, school dropout, rape, teenage pregnancies and early marriages, and the impunity of those who violate women. MEMPROW, which was started in 2008, is a feminist organisation that brings girls together in institutions of learning and out-of-school young women from across Uganda, to provide them with the skills and knowledge they need to become successful, confident, and self-reliant individuals.

MEMPROW was likened, by the girls and boys who are MEMPROW's primary stakeholders, to the "Kayora" (that which collects anything and everything) train of the 1980s, which collected everybody and took them to their different destinations in Kampala. Kayora Train did not discriminate,

---

[38] "The MEMPROW Train: How MEMPROW Transformed Me," a MEMPROW publication.

and even when it was full to the brim, there was always room for one more. Likewise, in MEMPROW, the stakeholders describe it as an organisation where everybody is welcome and there is always room for one more. But unlike the train, even when you do not know where you are going, MEMPROW helps you to get to a good place.

MEMPROW has focused particularly on mentoring and empowering girls and young women for improved performance and retention in various institutions, especially schools. What we have learned on this train journey, as we collected girls and boys, women and men and people with other gender identities, is that change is possible even in patriarchal mind-sets and practices. This is because we were able to understand the barriers and issues our stakeholders were dealing with. During this time, we came to understand how the problem of girls' poor attainment and retention especially is related to the systemic nature of sexual gender-based violence (SGBV) and lack of information on sexual reproductive health and rights. Further, the patriarchal socio-cultural framework that is so characteristic of Uganda in both formal and informal institutions unintentionally creates and provides space for subordination of girls and women in all public and private institutions. We were then able to design programme that respond to the issues and needs created in their specific environment. We were able to do this because all programmes designed at MEMPROW are preceded by stakeholder needs analysis.

Through the girls' voices, we at MEMPROW have come to:

1) Understand the diverse nature of violence and the absolute power of patriarchy in subordinating women and legitimising SGBV and gender inequalities. Today, we understand even more the pervasive and destructive nature of patriarchy when we talk to girls. Take, for example, a young girl who is being defiled by a father, and she is not willing to report because of the fear of the shame it will bring to her father.

2) Appreciate the power of voice and how it gives girls the power to identify and name the various forms of abuse they experience; this is contributing to eliminating the culture of silence. MEMPROW Girls are enabled to demystify their abusers; most times, it is those who are close with power and authority over them. For example, when girls are asked in the training sessions to role play some of their challenges, in one play they demonstrated domestic violence and how it is targeted at mothers and daughters by male members of the family. Sexual harassment from male teachers and fellow students; excessive domestic work combined with food deprivation; and the impacts of unwanted/unplanned pregnancies are issues that are constant in discussions with the girls.

3) Recognise that focusing on building girls' confidence and self-esteem is just half the job. Dismantling the power of patriarchal beliefs over the lives of girls and young women is the other half of the job that needs to be done.

4) Most importantly, through our work, we have come to appreciate the strength, resilience, and the capacity of the girls and young women we work with to forgive. They are engaged in battles almost every day of their lives: at home; on the way to and from school; and at school. They are fighting an enemy whose nature and identity they have no clue of. But they have survived because they have mastered social skills that only experience teaches. One time, we organized a workshop for forty girls from ten primary schools in Nebbi, Western Uganda, and a very poor part of the country. A thirteen-year-old girl, sobbing her heart out, narrated to us how every day before she goes to school, her grandfather, who is also her guardian, tells her she should get married and stop wasting his food. We all cried. But then she added on, "I go home every day and cook for him, even when he tells me not to come back," throwing all of us into roaring laughter.

Every encounter with each of the girls and the boys, for me, has been a lesson in endurance and forgiveness. And a true meaning of what it means to focus on the silver lining, in order to get to the end of the train journey.

I will end this narrative of my feminist journey, with a voice from a MEMPROW Girl, in a poem written to me as her farewell gift to me when I stepped out of MEMPROW as the Executive Director.

Dr. Hilda Tadria

She is a soft hearted warrior
She left between us and her no
barrier
She made us her very own
You'd think she were our biological
carrier

We moved from being worriers to
Warriors
It's no wonder they say it takes a
Community to raise a Child
Community is Empowering,
Community is a pillar
She was just that
..... our Community

I don't celebrate you only today, I've
celebrated you since I walked into
Memprow.

From Hawa Kimbugwe

My older brother, the firstborn child, Geoffrey and I getting ready for the nine-kilometre trek to school in the early 1950s. I believe this is where my train journey started and has continued with many exciting stops on the way.

As young children, in 1955, my elder brother and I enjoying and showing off our new Christmas wear.

Setting off from home with my father to Gayaza High School for my ordinary level education, a momentous occasion.

As a student in Makerere, I was a human rights activist already. This picture was taken after our Makerere University students' public demonstration against the Rhodesian (now Zimbabwe) Universal government's war against indigenous Rhodesians.

Life in Cambridge offered huge opportunities, including growing up to face challenges of a foreign culture.

Cambridge created an opportunity for my going to Minnesota.

Undaunted by a near-tragic accident, my husband and I had our wedding three weeks later, with an eye patch over my eye. Always determined to beat the odds.

Family vision guided our life choices

Patrice and Vanessa, our children, setting out to Nursery School

Contrary to negative perceptions about my parenting as a feminist working mother, our children grew up to finish university and become independent adults. Children's Graduation at Loughborough University

Celebrating our 25th wedding anniversary

Always an engaged parent, Mr. Tadria sharing a harvest moment with grandchildren

Family reunions are a treasure, and our adventures include facing Murchison National Park, Uganda

*Family reunions are a treasure, and our adventures include facing Murchison
National Park, Uganda*

*Family reunions are a treasure, and our adventures include facing Murchison
National Park, Uganda*

A family that eats together stays together.

Celebrating with grandchildren is a family tradition.

I got my passion for working with women, learned my community and social responsibility from my mother, who was never afraid to stand up and speak out. Here is a picture of her as a child bride at 16 years of age, 1941. Plucked out of school too early, she nevertheless emerged as a leader and stood for women's empowerment and rights.

My mother led in mobilising the community to invest in growing vegetables to combat poor nutrition.

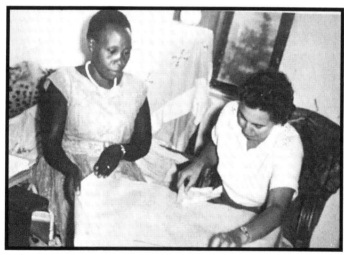

She was not afraid to sit at the table with other experts. Here she is with one of my teachers from Gayaza, in the sixties, discussing nutrition plans for her community.

In her later years, she represented her community at national political dialogues.

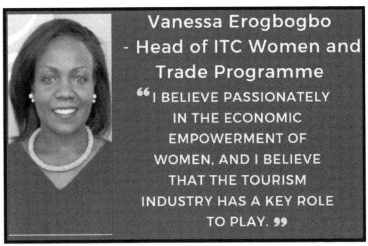

Vanessa Erogbogbo - Head of ITC Women and Trade Programme

"I BELIEVE PASSIONATELY IN THE ECONOMIC EMPOWERMENT OF WOMEN, AND I BELIEVE THAT THE TOURISM INDUSTRY HAS A KEY ROLE TO PLAY. "

My daughter, Vanessa, following in the footsteps of her foremothers

Patrice, wearing an apron and making birthday lunch for his son, who was turning fifteen years old

FURTHER READING & RESOURCES

Sylvia Tamale. *Decolonisation and Afro-Feminism*. Daraja Press: 2020.

"What is Feminism?" Owen M. Fiss, Yale Law School Legal Scholarship Repository Faculty Scholarship Series: Yale Law School Faculty Scholarship, 1-1-1994.

William Easterly. *The Tyranny of Experts: Economists, Dictators, and the Forgotten Rights of the Poor*. Published by Basic Books, 2013.

Robert Wyrod. *AIDS and Masculinity in the African City: Privilege, Inequality, and Modern Manhood*. University of California Press, 2016.

Michael McQueen. *The 'new' Rules of Engagement: A Guide to Understanding and Connecting with Generation Y*. First published by the Nexgen Group, 2007.

Paulo Freire. *Pedagogy of the Oppressed*. Published by Verlag Herder (as *Pedagogia do Oprimido)*, 1968; in English, 1970.

Hilda Mary Kabushenga Tadria. "Changing Economic and Gender Patterns among the Peasants of Ndejje and Sseguki in Uganda: a thesis submitted to the faculty of University of Minnesota," 1985.

Stephen Gudeman. *The Demise of a Rural Economy: From Subsistence to Capitalism in a Latin American Village*. Routlege and Kegan Paul, 1978.

T A Falaye, Ph.D. "Polygamy and Christianity in Africa." *Global Journal of Arts Humanities and Social Sciences*, Vol. 4, No. 10, pp.18-28. October 2016. Published by European Centre for Research Training and Development UK (www.eajournals.org) 18 ISSN: 2052-6350 (Print), 2052-6369 (Online). Department of Religious Studies Olabisi Onabanjo University, Ago-Iwoye Ogun State, Nigeria.

Deborah Tannen. *There is No Unmarked Woman*. Excerpt at: https://academics.otc.edu/media/uploads/sites/2/2015/10/There-is-No-Unmarked-Women.pdf.

Hope Chigudu. *MEMPROW Story: A Young Sister to the Women's Movement is Born! She is called MEMPROW*. A MEMPROW publication 2018

Jessica Horn. "Surviving COVID19: Why we need to listen to African women's Organisations." *https://medium.com/@AWDF/*

"The MEMPROW Train: How MEMPROW Transformed Me. Inspirational stories from young MEMPROW women and boys." A MEMPROW publication, 2015.

ABOUT THE AUTHOR

BORN IN KIGEZI, South West Uganda, Hilda Mary Kabushenga Tadria is a renowned passionate feminist and gender-equality activist who finally retired from active service in April 2020, exiting the role of Founding Executive Director of the Mentoring and Empowerment Programme for Young Women (MEMPROW), an organization based in Uganda that she started with her husband, Mr. Tadria, in January 2008. Hilda is also a co-founder and Board member of the African Women's Development Fund (AWDF), a fundraising and grant making organisation that supports women's work. In 1985, while still at Makerere, she founded Action for Development, an organisation that is still vibrant and active in protection of women's rights in Uganda.

Hilda has worked in diverse institutions, with a professional career lifespan of fifty years. She started as a Research Assistant at the Makerere Institute of Social Research in 1970, immediately after obtaining her first degree. She rose to the position of Associate Professor in Sociology at Makerere University before joining the Eastern and Southern African Management Institute (ESAMI) as a Senior Consultant and coordinator of the Women in

Development Programme. She left to join the Africa Capacity Building Foundation as a Programme Officer.

She has also worked as an international consultant on gender and development in many organisations, such as the World Bank, UNDP, UNIFEM and governments within the Africa region, before joining the United Nations Economic Commission for Africa, where she worked as a Regional Advisor on Economic Empowerment of Women.

Dr. Tadria holds a first-class degree in Sociology from the University of East Africa, a master's degree in Social Anthropology from Newnham College, Cambridge University, England, and a doctorate degree in Social Anthropology and Women's Studies from the University of Minnesota, USA. She has technical competencies in Capacity-Building for Social Development, Gender Mainstreaming Strategies and Processes (such as Gender Training, Gender and Development Policy design and Analysis), Gender and Development Needs and Social Impact assessments, Programme/Project Evaluation, Process Consultancy, Project Design, Participatory Training, and Meetings Facilitation. She also has extensive knowledge of many African countries, having worked directly in Ethiopia, Kenya, Uganda, Tanzania, Zambia, Zimbabwe, Swaziland, Botswana, Lesotho, Malawi, Mauritius, Namibia, South Africa, Seychelles, Ghana, Rwanda, Eritrea.

Hilda's major influence has been in developing organisational management capacities, gender responsive policies, mentoring girls and young women into leadership, and working to dismantle institutionalised systemic discrimination and violence against girls and women in

Africa. For her work, she has received awards in recognition of her contribution to the Girl Child education from Federation of Women Educators and Plan International (Uganda Chapters); and from International Planned Parenthood Federation (AFRICA), for her advocacy work for women's access to sexual and reproductive health and rights.

In 2019, she received from the Uganda Government a Medal of Honour for her work in promoting girls' and women's rights. In 2012, she was described as a Heroine and one of the fifty women in Uganda who made a difference. (*Sunday Vision*, 04/03/2012).

Dr. Tadria has served on several national and international Boards including:

International Crops Research Institute for the Semi-Arid Tropics (ICRISAT) based in Hyderabad, India, 1993-1999.

Advisory Board Member – National Long-Term Perspective Studies (NLTPS) UNDP.

Advisory Group member – Africa 2000 Network, UNDP.

Member of Civil Society Technical Advisory Group for the African Capacity Building Foundation in Harare.

Advisory Group member – UNIFEM Project on Building Technical capacity, Kenya.

Member of Local Advisory Board: ISIS-WICCE International, Uganda.

Board Member, Centre for Basic Research, Kampala, Uganda.

Printed in Great Britain
by Amazon